D0208950

VERY SHORT INTRODUCTIONS are for anyone wanting a stimulating and accessible way in to a new subject. They are written by experts and have been translated into more than 40 different languages. The series began in 1995 and now covers a wide variety of topics in every discipline. The VSI library contains nearly 400 volumes—a Very Short Introduction to everything from Indian philosophy to psychology and American history—and continues to grow in every subject area.

Very Short Introductions available now:

ADVERTISING Winston Fletcher
AFRICAN HISTORY
    John Parker and Richard Rathbone
AGNOSTICISM Robin Le Poidevin
AMERICAN HISTORY Paul S. Boyer
AMERICAN IMMIGRATION
    David A. Gerber
AMERICAN POLITICAL PARTIES AND
    ELECTIONS L. Sandy Maisel
AMERICAN POLITICS Richard M. Valelly
THE AMERICAN PRESIDENCY
    Charles O. Jones
ANAESTHESIA Aidan O'Donnell
ANARCHISM Colin Ward
ANCIENT EGYPT Ian Shaw
ANCIENT GREECE Paul Cartledge
ANCIENT PHILOSOPHY Julia Annas
ANCIENT WARFARE Harry Sidebottom
ANGELS David Albert Jones
ANGLICANISM Mark Chapman
THE ANGLO-SAXON AGE John Blair
THE ANIMAL KINGDOM Peter Holland
ANIMAL RIGHTS David DeGrazia
THE ANTARCTIC Klaus Dodds
ANTISEMITISM Steven Beller
ANXIETY Daniel Freeman and Jason Freeman
THE APOCRYPHAL GOSPELS Paul Foster
ARCHAEOLOGY Paul Bahn
ARCHITECTURE Andrew Ballantyne
ARISTOCRACY William Doyle
ARISTOTLE Jonathan Barnes
ART HISTORY Dana Arnold
ART THEORY Cynthia Freeland
ASTROBIOLOGY David C. Catling
ATHEISM Julian Baggini
AUGUSTINE Henry Chadwick
AUSTRALIA Kenneth Morgan
AUTISM Uta Frith
THE AVANT GARDE David Cottington
THE AZTECS David Carrasco
BACTERIA Sebastian G. B. Amyes

BARTHES Jonathan Culler
THE BEATS David Sterritt
BEAUTY Roger Scruton
BESTSELLERS John Sutherland
THE BIBLE John Riches
BIBLICAL ARCHAEOLOGY Eric H. Cline
BIOGRAPHY Hermione Lee
THE BLUES Elijah Wald
THE BOOK OF MORMON Terryl Givens
BORDERS
    Alexander C. Diener and Joshua Hagen
THE BRAIN Michael O'Shea
THE BRITISH CONSTITUTION
    Martin Loughlin
THE BRITISH EMPIRE Ashley Jackson
BRITISH POLITICS Anthony Wright
BUDDHA Michael Carrithers
BUDDHISM Damien Keown
BUDDHIST ETHICS Damien Keown
CANCER Nicholas James
CAPITALISM James Fulcher
CATHOLICISM Gerald O'Collins
CAUSATION
    Stephen Mumford and Rani Lill Anjum
THE CELL Terence Allenand Graham Cowling
THE CELTS Barry Cunliffe
CHAOS Leonard Smith
CHILDREN'S LITERATURE
    Kimberley Reynolds
CHINESE LITERATURE Sabina Knight
CHOICE THEORY Michael Allingham
CHRISTIAN ART Beth Williamson
CHRISTIAN ETHICS D. Stephen Long
CHRISTIANITY Linda Woodhead
CITIZENSHIP Richard Bellamy
CIVIL ENGINEERING David Muir Wood
CLASSICAL MYTHOLOGY Helen Morales
CLASSICS Mary Beard and John Henderson
CLAUSEWITZ Michael Howard
CLIMATE Mark Maslin
THE COLD WAR Robert McMahon

Islamic History: A Very Short Introduction

Adam J. Silverstein

ISLAMIC HISTORY

A Very Short Introduction

OXFORD
UNIVERSITY PRESS

OXFORD
UNIVERSITY PRESS

Great Clarendon Street, Oxford ox2 6DP

Oxford University Press is a department of the University of Oxford.
It furthers the University's objective of excellence in research, scholarship,
and education by publishing worldwide in

Oxford New York

Auckland Cape Town Dar es Salaam Hong Kong Karachi
Kuala Lumpur Madrid Melbourne Mexico City Nairobi
New Delhi Shanghai Taipei Toronto

With offices in

Argentina Austria Brazil Chile Czech Republic France Greece
Guatemala Hungary Italy Japan Poland Portugal Singapore
South Korea Switzerland Thailand Turkey Ukraine Vietnam

Oxford is a registered trade mark of Oxford University Press
in the UK and in certain other countries

Published in the United States
by Oxford University Press Inc., New York

British Library Cataloguing in Publication Data

Data available

Library of Congress Cataloging in Publication Data

Data available

Typeset by SPI Publisher Services, Pondicherry, India
Printed in Great Britain by
Ashford Colour Press Ltd, Gosport, Hampshire

ISBN 978-0-19-954572-8

5 7 9 10 8 6

In Memoriam
Michael Fox (1934–2009)

Contents

Acknowledgements

This book largely reflects the contents of lecture courses on Islamic history that I have taught at the universities of Cambridge and Oxford. Though teaching at such esteemed universities is undoubtedly a privilege, the experience can also be a 'school of hard knocks' for a young lecturer trying out new ideas. My students, who were routinely brighter and better prepared than I was, never let me get away with anything unclear or half-baked. For their input over the years I am very grateful to them all and in particular to Imogen Ware who prepared the book's Index.

I also wish to thank my colleagues Anna Akasoy, Patricia Crone, David Powers, and Chase Robinson who kindly read early drafts of the book and saved me from numerous errors of fact and judgement.

I would like to thank Luciana O'Flaherty and Andrea Keegan for commissioning the book, Emma Marchant, Kerstin Demata, and Keira Dickinson for seeing it through the process of publication, and Erica Martin for help with the illustrations.

Finally, the mushy bit: My parents and my wife, Sophie, read a draft of the book and gave me many helpful comments on it.

But they have also given me just about everything else that is important in life and I cannot quite think how to thank them for it all. And if I ever seem to them to be lost in thought they should know that I'm merely struggling to think of ways to make it up to them. Or thinking about work.

Preface

In recent years it has become increasingly obvious to non-Muslim Westerners that Islam matters. Whether or not this is a good thing continues to occupy a central place in public debates and in the media. On the basis of some of their recent statements, Prince Charles appears to be a fan; Pope Benedict XVI – not so much. The growing visibility of Muslims in newspaper headlines and on the streets of European and North American cities has raised important issues concerning integration, multiculturalism, interfaith relations, and even what it means to be 'British', 'American', or 'Western' altogether. Do headscarves and veils have a place in modern Western societies or do they – as a British foreign minister and the French government have suggested – obstruct communication and threaten our 'core values' and security?

Regardless of one's opinions on these matters, it is clear to many that there is a conflict brewing between 'Islam' and the Judeo-Christian culture upon which Western civilization is thought to be based. But why should this be so? After all, Islam is a form of monotheism that arose in the midst of predominantly Jewish and Christian communities in the Near East. And when the first Muslims spread beyond Arabia's borders, some contemporary Christians assumed that they were Jews, and some Jews thought they were Christians. How then are we to explain the enormous cultural gulf that appears to separate Judeo-Christian, Western societies from Muslim ones?

To answer this question we must turn to Islamic history. The role that Islamic history plays in modern Muslim societies is extremely important, though it is often overlooked since it has no equivalent in the modern West. For this reason, understanding the rise and subsequent development of Islam may enable us to interpret modern Muslim societies and understand their relation to – and relationship with – Western ones.

List of illustrations

Introduction

This book is about the story, study, and significance of Islamic history. The following chapters will attempt to answer three questions about the subject: What happened? (Chapters 1 to 3); How do we know this? (Chapters 4 and 5); and Why does it matter? (Chapters 6 and 7). First, however, we must consider an even bigger question – What *is* Islamic history? Is it the history of those places where Muslims have been in power? Or is it the history of Muslims wherever they are and have been? Perhaps it is the history that is important to Muslims – if we were to ask a pre-modern Muslim to define the limits of Islamic history he would likely be puzzled by the suggestion that it has temporal or spatial limits at all. According to Islamic tradition, Adam, Noah, Abraham, Moses, Alexander the Great, and Jesus were all Muslims; in fact, they are all considered prophets (yes, Alexander too).

Muslim historians such as al-Tabari (d. 923), who had purely religious concerns in mind, begin their study of history with God's creation of the world, some 6,500 years before Muhammad's birth, according to their reckoning. Another 'Islamic' approach is to take Muhammad's emigration (*hijra*) from Mecca to Medina in 622 as the starting point: this, as we will see, is when the Muslim calendar begins, though it would be difficult to argue that the years between 610 and 622, when Muhammad was

1. Alexander the Great visiting the Ka'ba in Mecca

receiving revelations (and the new faith was receiving converts), do not count somehow. According to the reckoning adopted in what follows, Islamic history began in the 7th century. It should, however, be borne in mind from the outset that, as with most questions to be posed in this book, the answer is: 'It depends whom you ask'. From the 7th century onwards, the history that is taken to be 'Islamic' is that in which Islam was a politically, religiously, or culturally dominant force.

Islamic history is the product of people and their actions. But people in the pre-modern world were the product of their environment. They could not ignore the natural backdrop against which the events of Islamic history unfolded and nor can we.

Geography

Islam nowadays is everywhere. Until the early modern period, however, it was *somewhere*, in particular the lands between the Atlantic in the west and Central Asia in the east. The region is sometimes referred to as the Great Arid Zone, as the cold (Siberian) air from the north and east of the region together with the hot (Saharan) air from the south and west combined over time to create an inhospitably dry interior. Much of the Arabian Peninsula, Syria, Iran, and elsewhere is desert and the Great Arid Zone as a whole is predominantly arid or semi-arid.

To the problems posed by a dry climate there are two basic solutions: find water resources aside from rain, or find ways of living that do not depend too heavily on water. Both options have been tried in Islamic history. The region's inadequate rainwater has been supplemented by irrigation systems, including natural ones such as the Nile's annual flooding as well as man-made canals, reservoirs, and subterranean tunnel-wells (*qanat*s) that have guided the Tigris, Euphrates, and Iran's rivers (as well as what exists of the region's rainwater) to fertile destinations since

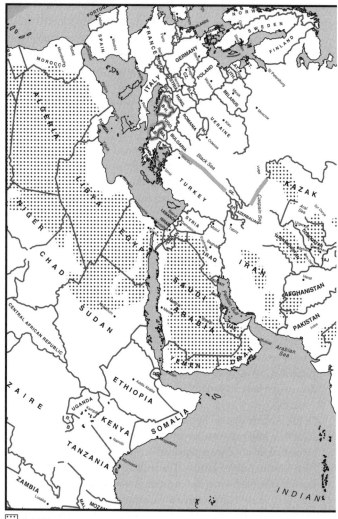

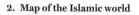

Islamic History

:::: Arid Zone

2. Map of the Islamic world

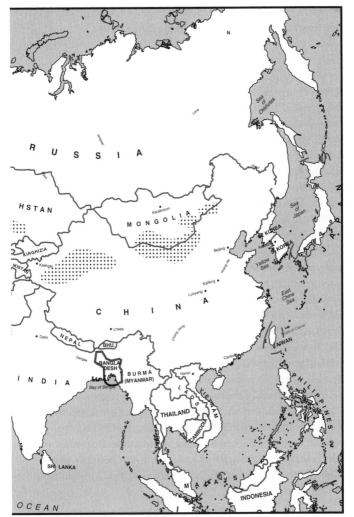

ancient times. These systems present their own set of problems in that they are difficult to maintain and easy to disrupt.

The second solution to the region's aridity, which benefited riverless regions such as Arabia, is none other than the trusty camel, whose impact on Arabian society in the 6th century, on the spread of Islam in the 7th, and on the shape of Muslim towns and cities in the 8th to 11th centuries was considerable. What camels have going for them is their incredible ability to cope with short supplies over long periods; they are thus economically efficient and low-maintenance. What they have going against them is that their sensitive feet cannot cope with cold or uneven terrain. Muhammad may have gone to the mountain, but his immediate successors did no such thing, at least not to begin with, and throughout Islamic history mountain ranges have proven – by chance or by design – to be safe havens for those seeking to withstand pressure to convert, conform, or cooperate more generally. On account of their relative inaccessibility, mountains have helped locals as well as newcomers seeking refuge to retain their religious traditions (Christians in northern Spain, Anatolia, Armenia, Lebanon, and the Ethiopian highlands; and Zoroastrians and other dualists in northern Iran), and their cultural traditions (Persian in Iran, Berber in North Africa, Kurdish in northern Iraq), just as they were exploited by those escaping the reach of the central authorities more generally (Ismailis in Syria and northern Iran, Zaydis in Yemen, and the Taliban in Afghanistan). It is not for nothing that Moroccan political authorities referred to their mountainous regions as '*siba*', [the lands of] rebellion. Soviet and latterly American troops in Afghanistan learned these facts the hard way; local Muslims have known them all along.

Not all camels are deterred by mountains, however: two-humped Bactrian camels are hardier than Arabia's single-humped dromedaries. When, from the 11th century, large numbers of Turkic nomads made their way from Central Asia westwards into the Near East, the mountains of northern Iran and Anatolia (and the relatively cold climate in these regions) did little to halt their advance, for which reason what was then 'Anatolia' is now 'Turkey'. It was amongst the Arabs in the 7th century, though, that Islam arose and it is with Arabs – and their dromedaries – that it first spread. That most of the arid and semi-arid zones of the Old World were swiftly conquered by Arabs bearing a new religion is not surprising; nor is the fact that the limits of their advance were partly set by climate – the humid conditions in Europe may have been just as effective a barrier to the advance of Islam as local armies were.

But why didn't the Arabs just stay in Arabia? After all, they had done so for quite a long time and their pre-Islamic poetry depicts a society that knew about the settled civilizations of their neighbours but did not aspire to join them: rugged manliness was celebrated by the Arabs; silk robes and signet rings were for wimps. Nobody in the year 600 could have predicted that within a short century, the uncouth, lizard-eating Arabs (as non-Arab Muslims called them centuries later) would rule an enormous empire from palaces in Damascus and, later, Baghdad. And although there are well over a billion Muslims worldwide today, in the year 600 there were none; what happened in between is the subject of the next chapter.

Chapter 1
The story

600–800 CE

According to both Muslim tradition and most modern historians, Islam began in Arabia. To Muslims this happened not with Muhammad but with Abraham, who – together with his son Ishmael, the progenitor of the Arabs – built the Ka'ba in Mecca to which millions of Muslims have gone on pilgrimage until today. Modern historians skip over this and start with Muhammad's career in Mecca, and we too will begin there.

The Arabian Peninsula is a big place and is suitably varied – ethnically, topographically, culturally, and, on the eve of Islam, religiously. The bit of Arabia that concerns us most is the western region known as the Hijaz, which is where Mecca and Medina are situated. Muhammad was born in Mecca c. 570 into the town's leading tribe (Quraysh), though he was from a relatively minor branch of the tribe and was orphaned at a young age. In 610, at the age of 40, he began to receive revelations that would become verses of the Quran, which he shared with his friends and family, and eventually with others in Mecca. His monotheistic message was inconsistent with the town's polytheistic culture and, in 622, he was forced to flee, together with his supporters. He came to settle in Medina, an oasis populated by – among others – a large number of Jews, where his message about God, past prophets, the end of days, fasting, charity, and the like, was familiar and unthreatening. He was welcomed in the town where he served as an adjudicator for some disputes that had been dividing the population. This emigration (*hijra*) is the starting point of both Muhammad's career as a statesman and of the Muslim calendar.

From his base in Medina, Muhammad set about establishing a new community (*umma*) made up of fellow emigrants from Mecca and those in Medina who supported him. For the next ten years, Muhammad continued to receive revelations, which often bore direct relevance to the *umma*'s needs and circumstances and reflected its growing power and confidence. Muhammad's dealings with the Meccan pagans and the Medinese Jews dominate accounts of the Medinese phase of his career: as his relations with the Jews soured, their tribes were gradually expelled from the town and even, in one instance, executed. The Meccans were eventually defeated in 630 and over the next two years Muhammad managed to unite the tribes of Arabia under the *umma*'s banner. His successes were widely taken as a sign of divine favour, and must have encouraged tribes throughout Arabia to cooperate and convert. Divine favour aside, Muhammad is described in early sources as a mortal who lived as an ordinary, even fallible human being (God rebukes him repeatedly in the Quran, though later Islamic tradition would come to hold that he had been infallible), and in 632 he died as one.

Muhammad's death set off two chain reactions whose consequences were momentous, in the one case leading to the emergence of Islamic sects and in the other to the emergence of an Islamic empire. In the first chain reaction, certain groups considered the Prophet's death to be the beginning of an era; in the second, some other groups saw it as the end of one. It was the beginning of an era for those Muslims who submitted to the rule of the caliph or 'successor', who acceded to leadership of the *umma* shortly after Muhammad's death. The reign of the first caliph, Abu Bakr (r. 632–4), was mostly spent dealing with the second chain reaction.

It was the end of an era for those tribes whose conversion to Islam had been inextricably linked to Muhammad himself; now that he was dead, they reasoned, their contract with him was void. Some tribes retained their new religious identity (which was fine) but withheld their taxes and allegiance from the *umma* (which was not). Other tribes also reverted to their pre-Islamic religions (shifting religious allegiances was common in pagan Arabia). All such groups were deemed to be political and religious apostates, whose return to the fold was crucial. The ensuing 'wars of apostasy' (*ridda*) succeeded not only in achieving their basic aims but also in creating the momentum and need for conquests beyond the peninsula. Many Arabians were pastoral nomads, and like other pastoral nomads, they relied to a significant extent on raiding others for their livelihood. The unification of Arabia's numerous tribes under a new religious banner instilled in them a new sense of social cohesion and a spiritual purpose that harnessed the nomadic need to raid (which was merged with *jihad*, to which we will return in Chapter 3), while also depriving the Arabs of obvious victims: because Muslims could not raid each other, they raided their neighbours in Syria, Egypt, North Africa, Iraq, and Iran.

These raids were different, however. For the first time, rather than just looting the settled peoples of the Near East, the nomads actually brought them something of their own: a new religious message. Neither the Byzantine rulers in the west, nor the Sasanid rulers in the east, wanted it (according to tradition, already in Muhammad's day letters were sent to imperial leaders inviting them to Islam); their subjects, however, were more receptive – if not always to the religion itself then at least to Muslim hegemony.

That the conquests of the Near East were as impressive to contemporaries as they are to us is evidenced by the fact that both the conquerors and the conquered were certain that God's hand must have been guiding events – Muslims interpreted their success as God's reward to them for following His will; Christians

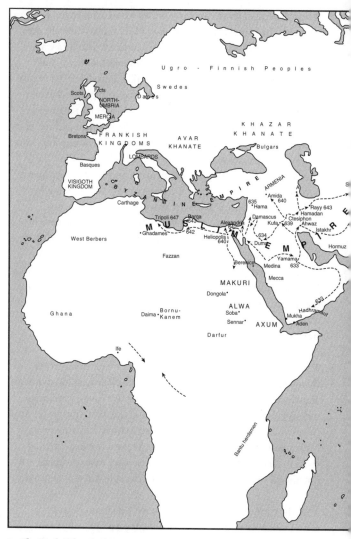

3. The Early Islamic Conquests

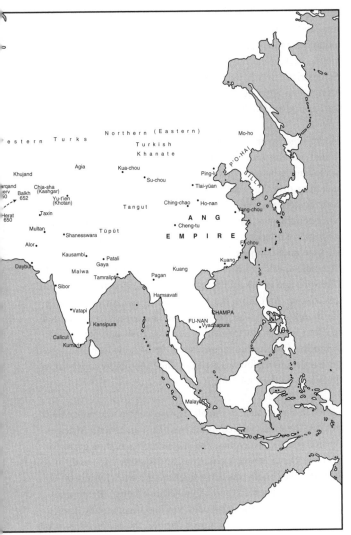

estern Turks

Northern (Eastern)
Turkish
Khanate

Mo-ho

P'O-HAI

SILLA

Khujand

Agia

Kua-chou

Ping-lu

Su-chou

Tlai-yüan

arqand
erv
50
Herat
650

Chia-sha
(Kashgar)
Balkh
652

Yu-t'ien
(Khotan)

Ching-chao

Ho-nan

Yang-chou

Taxin

Tangut

A N G

Cheng-tu

Multan

Shanesswara

Tüpüt

E M P I R E

Fu-chou

Alor

Kausambi

Patali

Kuang

Daybul

Malwa

Tamralipt

Gaya

Pagan

Kuang

Sibor

Hamsavati

Vatapi

Kansipura

CHAMPA

FU-NAN

Vyadhapura

Calicut

Kumari

Malayu

13

were certain that their failures were God's retribution for their sins; and some Jews saw Islam as part of God's plan to spread monotheism to remote pagans of the Hijaz, or as a fulfilment of messianic expectations. (We do not know for certain what the Zoroastrians in Iran made of the rise of Islam, but they must have been unhappy about it, having lost the support and patronage that the Sasanid empire had hitherto offered them.)

Modern historians look elsewhere for explanations and have settled on three basic theories. First, the imperial powers were weak, having battled each other to a costly and exhausting stalemate over the preceding centuries. Second, much of the Near Eastern population was eager to exchange its rulers for more benign ones, having accumulated various grievances over centuries of religiously and economically unpopular policies. That the first lands conquered were inhabited by Semitic monotheists (Aramaic-speaking Christians and Jews in Byzantine Syria and Palestine, and in Sasanid Iraq) must also have been significant in this context. And third, the Arabs had military advantages over the Byzantine and Sasanid armies, and managed to exploit their religious fervour, the element of surprise, their familiarity with Byzantine and Sasanid tactics (some Arabs previously had served the empires in military capacities), and their ability to retreat to the desert on their mounts.

Which brings us back to camels. Howsoever we rationalize their success, the Arabs arrived in the Near East and North Africa in the mid to late 7th century, and stayed there, creating garrison towns in North Africa, Egypt, Iraq, and eastern Iran – only in Syria did the conquerors settle in existing towns (joining other Arabs who had settled there in pre-Islamic times). By the end of the 8th century, the garrison towns had become fully fledged cities and the Arabs had ventured out into towns and cities of the Near East, leaving a lasting mark on the landscape: the spread of camel breeding throughout the conquered territories accelerated the process by which the inefficient and high-maintenance wheeled vehicles, which required paved roads, were replaced by the simpler and more economical Arabian camels. In provinces conquered from the Byzantine empire, straight, wide Roman roads gave way to the windy and narrow streets still seen in the old quarters of Near Eastern cities whose layout was influenced both by the absence of a distinctively public realm in early Islamic cities and by the spread of this unique Arabian 'technology'. These garrison towns themselves became important economic hubs, drawing to them non-Muslims from neighbouring settlements, and redrawing the map of the Near East.

It was the spread of Arabic and Islam, however, that represents the most significant consequence of the early conquests. While the pivotal victories over the empires occurred during the reign of the second caliph, 'Umar (r. 634–44), it was under the Umayyad caliphs (r. 661–750) that Arabic culture and Islamic rule spread – to some degree or another – from the Iberian Peninsula to the Punjab, more or less fixing the frontiers of the Islamic world for centuries to come.

To some Muslims in the late 7th century, and to almost all Muslims since then, the Umayyads should not have been caliphs at all. Their four predecessors – Abu Bakr, 'Umar, 'Uthman (r. 644–56), and 'Ali (r. 656–61) – had all been related to Muhammad either by marriage or by blood (or both, in 'Ali's case), and the reign of these four caliphs, known (to Sunnis in subsequent centuries) as 'Rightly Guided Ones' (*rashidun*), is remembered as having been a sort of Golden Age during which the *umma* was governed according to 'Islamic' principles. ('Shiites' are those who believe that 'Ali should have succeeded Muhammad immediately.) The Umayyads, by contrast, were not directly related to the Prophet and, moreover, are said to have resisted him openly, only converting out of necessity, relatively late in Muhammad's career. Although 'Uthman himself was of the Umayyad family, he had converted early on, was Muhammad's son-in-law, and is credited (though, to some at the time, discredited) with ordering the assembly of an authoritative version of the Quran – amongst other good deeds. Things began to go wrong when 'Uthman was murdered, and two claimants to the caliphal office emerged: 'Ali – whose supporters had been championing his candidacy since 632; and Mu'awiya – an Umayyad kinsman of 'Uthman's who demanded the right to avenge 'Uthman's blood. 'Ali became caliph in 656 and struggled to exert his influence widely; by 657, he had entered into negotiations with Mu'awiya. To many of 'Ali's supporters, this should never have happened – 'Judgement belongs to God alone', was their slogan – and they seceded from his camp, for which reason they are known as 'seceders' or 'Kharijites'. Their strongly held views on the right to rule impelled them to deem dissenters as infidels worthy of death. Their most high-profile victim was 'Ali himself in 661, though Kharijite groups would continue to oppose the caliphs for the next century and beyond.

With 'Ali's death, the age of 'Rightly Guided' caliphs ended. The bloody rivalry that led to Mu'awiya's accession came to be known as the first Civil War or *fitna* ('strife') in Islamic history, marking the end of a period of perceived unity within the *umma*. The Umayyads were thus off to a bad start and, according to sources written by those hostile to them, things continued to get worse. Mu'awiya moved the capital to Damascus and designated his son Yazid (r. 680–3) as his successor, thereby establishing the principle of hereditary succession – for which the Umayyads were criticized (by those, it should be added, who created dynasties themselves). Yazid ran into trouble early on – killing 'Ali's son Hussein at Karbala (Iraq) in 680, which has cemented his infamy in the minds of Shiites – and his authority was challenged by another caliph in the Hijaz. Neither Yazid nor his son Mu'awiya II (r. 683) lasted long. A second *fitna* caused great disruption at this time (680–92), and it is only with the reign of 'Abd al-Malik (r. 692–705) that Umayyad sovereignty was restored; 692 became known as a 'year of unity' and administrative measures were taken to tighten the caliph's control over his subjects, to prevent future challenges to his authority.

'Abd al-Malik and his successors, though generally maligned in our sources as being impious kings (rather than pious caliphs), are grudgingly acknowledged as having made lasting contributions to Islamic civilization. They imposed Arabic as the official administrative language in Islamic lands, and extended these lands as far west as Spain and Morocco, and as far east as Pakistan and Central Asia. The caliph's control over his provinces was tightened – with decentralized, tribal traditions giving way to better-organized imperial ones – and a consciously Arabic and Islamic identity was developed and imposed on caliphal institutions. 'Islamic' coins were minted, Arabic replaced Greek, Persian, and Coptic in administrative bureaus (opening the door to Muslim participation), and – most strikingly – the Dome of the Rock was constructed on the Temple Mount in Jerusalem, confronting (or, to some scholars, meeting) Judaism's messianic expectations and bearing an inscription that challenges Christianity's basic doctrines. The point was clear for all to see: Islam had arrived.

But what did 'Islam' mean in this period? The Umayyads' biggest problem was that their answer to this question differed fundamentally from that of the (self-appointed) religious scholars, the *'ulama'* (sing. *'alim*) as they would come to be known, who commanded popular support at the time, and who wrote the history books later on. For the Umayyads, Muhammad's death was indeed the end of an era – as Muhammad was the 'seal' of prophets, God's will would no longer be communicated through men bearing scriptures. Instead, it was the caliphs who served as His representatives on earth. This was the era of caliphs and it was they who possessed religious authority. To the religious scholars, this was nonsense. God provided the *umma* with all it needed to know: whatever was not in the Quran could be inferred from Muhammad's own statements and actions. Since nobody knew more about these things than the *'ulama'* themselves, religious authority should rest with them.

4. The Dome of the Rock, Jerusalem. Inscriptions on the building's octagonal arcade include Quranic verses that challenge some of the basic doctrines of Christianity

Unfortunately for the Umayyads, not only did a decisive proportion of their Muslim subjects side with the scholars, but many other Muslims had their own theological objections to their claim to the caliphate. Moreover, for much of the period (with one or two exceptions), conversion of the conquered peoples to Islam was discouraged by the caliphs, which meant two things: yet more people resented them (non-Muslims paid more taxes), and a majority of the caliphs' subjects were non-Muslim. Arab Muslims, non-Arab Muslims, Arab non-Muslims, and non-Arab non-Muslims all had cause to oppose the caliphs in Damascus. In 750, they were overthrown by what was basically a 'Shiite' revolt from the East that brought the Abbasid dynasty to the throne.

The Abbasids (750–1258) claimed descent from one of Muhammad's uncles and promised – in words and through select actions – to make a dramatic break with Umayyad injustices. They moved the centre of power from Syria to the east, building a new capital at Baghdad in 762, and adopted messianic titles, which were meant to indicate that business was *not* as usual. Of course in many ways it was: as the Umayyads before them, they too shed the blood of charismatic Muslim leaders (the architects of their own revolution were brutally murdered), established a dynasty, and – as far as we can tell – claimed religious authority for themselves. They also intensified the transition from a loose, tribally based state into a sophisticated empire. 'Abd al-Malik had begun this process half a century beforehand, but he had done so in Damascus, a city that, despite its formidable antiquity, had never been the seat of an empire. In Baghdad, the Abbasids were down the road from the old Sasanid capital of Ctesiphon, and although superficially the wine-women-and-song of pre-Islamic Arabia seems no different to the wine-women-and-song of the Abbasid court, by the reign of Harun al-Rashid (r. 786–809), the Near East had in many ways been set on a path that would see it transformed beyond recognition.

800–1100

That Islam exists at all is due to events in the 600–800 period. That it looks the way it does now is largely due to events in the 800–1100 one. And just as camels represented the first period, caravans can be said to represent the second one. A caravan consists of many camels (or other pack animals) led together by a group of travellers, which reflects one of the major differences between the Umayyads and the early Abbasids: the former created a somewhat exclusive, 'Arab' empire whereas the latter were consciously cosmopolitan and inclusive, empowering non-Arabs (mainly those who were culturally Persian – appropriately, 'caravan' is a Persian word) and absorbing them into Islam. Caravans are also central to this period for plying the routes that linked the Abbasids' sprawling provinces, transporting pilgrims, envoys, merchants, scholars, and soldiers across a road network that encouraged a level of internationalism, multiculturalism, and inter-connectivity that most Westerners would associate with modernity.

The foundations of this achievement are strikingly similar to those that are credited with the emergence of the modern West. But instead of a printing revolution, the Islamic world in this period experienced a paper revolution, whereby more expensive and elitist methods of writing (on papyrus and parchment, for example) were replaced by this more affordable medium. Literacy is thought to have increased dramatically, creating new readerships that consumed (and, in a circular way, generated) new genres of literature. Everything from pre-Islamic poetry to works on theology, philosophy, medicine, science, *belles-lettres*, and history was recorded in written form. A commensurate eruption in Islamic culture and civilization resulted, producing a diverse civilian elite in the Islamic world by the 9th century.

Travel and trade also flourished in this period, feeding from and into this cultural efflorescence. It is not just that travelogues (both real and imagined), maps, and geographies were produced on the basis of new experiences in far-flung lands – though this certainly happened – but also that Near Eastern merchants expanded their remit and horizons well beyond Abbasid borders. One 9th-century writer tells us of polyglot Iraqi Jews who criss-crossed Eurasia, travelling between France and China (covering Muslim lands, southern Russia, and India along the way), and the discovery of thousands of Abbasid coins in Scandinavia attests to the scope of this commercial activity. Even the spread of papermaking from China to the Near East is instructive in this context: our sources tell us that Muslims defeated a Chinese army in 751, capturing papermakers in the process from whom they learned the techniques themselves. What is interesting is that such hostile circumstances – a bloody battle in Central Asia – did little to hinder cross-cultural interaction and the spread of commodities, people, and ideas. Muslims in this period had active frontiers in

Spain, southern Europe, Central Asia, India, and Africa, affording both rulers and individuals the opportunity to derive kudos from waging *jihad*. The story about Chinese papermakers (and it is almost certainly just a story) reminds us that such confrontations were seen by the story's authors to present further occasions for cultural interaction as much as they stifled it.

This 'Golden Age' (as some have called it) of Islamic civilization was enabled by a delicate balance of appropriate circumstances, specifically the steady flow of income into the caliphal Treasury, supported by efficient book-keeping and the existence of relative stability within Abbasid lands. The equilibrium was disturbed from the second half of the 9th century onwards and the conditions for Abbasid globalization would never recover. The wealth brought in through trade and taxation began to diminish for a number of reasons. The carefully maintained Sawad region of southern Iraq from which the Abbasids derived much of their agricultural yield was plunged into chaos by a Kharijite-inspired revolt of East African slaves working in Basra (the '*Zanj*', 869–83). And governors in distant regions began to invest taxation revenues locally instead of sending the money to the capital, with economic independence often being followed by political independence. Furthermore, this is the period in which extensive conversion of non-Arabs to Islam resulted in the happy consequence of Islam's spread but also in the unhappy consequence of decreasing poll-tax revenues. To make matters worse, what was left in the coffers was quickly frittered away by a spendthrift court that expanded well beyond its capabilities and needs, creating new ruling elites who were often costlier than they were functional. It is in this period that the Abbasids came to lose political, military, and religious authority, as follows.

Politically, the Abbasids struggled to keep their extensive realms unified; with an empire that stretched some 6,500 kilometres from east to west, and without the benefits of modern communications, it was likely that some of their subjects would seek a measure of independence. Swift couriers, pigeons, beacons, and other methods of communication could to an extent cover the empire's enormous breadth, but political fragmentation was probably only a matter of time. In fact, in the case of Andalusia, it was not even that: already during the Abbasid takeover, an Umayyad prince fled to the Iberian Peninsula and established an independent state there, which – under 'Abd al-Rahman III (r. 912–61) and his successors – would become a 'caliphate', and a magnificent centre of high culture. When the Abbasids transferred power and attention to the east, the western provinces of the caliphate gradually broke away: Morocco under the Idrisids (789–926), the rest of North Africa under the Aghlabids (800–909), Egypt under the Tulunids (868–905) and Ikhshidids (935–69), to be followed by the Fatimid caliphs in North Africa, Egypt, and Syria (909–1171). Even the eastern provinces sought a measure of independence, with the Tahirids ruling in Khurasan (821–73), followed there by the Samanids (874–1005) and the Ghaznavids (977–1186), who were based in eastern Afghanistan. With one or two exceptions (such as the Saffarids in eastern Iran, 861–900) these eastern dynasties tended to cooperate with and formally recognize the Abbasid authorities; western dynasties such as the Idrisids, Andalusian Umayyads, and Fatimids did not. In practice, however, for purely geographical reasons, the Abbasids often had more interaction – both positive and negative – with disloyal Egypt and Syria than with nominally loyal eastern Iran and Central Asia.

Militarily, in the early 9th century the Abbasids began to replace the army that brought them to power with Turkish slave-soldiers (*mamluk*s or *ghulam*s) purchased or captured from Central Asia. These Turks had three attractions for the caliph al-Mu'tasim (r. 833–42), who was the first to import them in large numbers. First, being outsiders, they were not concerned with local allegiances or popular pressures; their loyalty was to the caliph himself. Second, they were excellent mounted archers who had military advantages over the Khurasani troops whom they replaced. And third, their status as Turkic slaves – though they were converted to Islam and often manumitted – meant that they could never lay claim to the caliphal office. In theory, slave-soldiers were a great idea; in practice, they quickly got out of hand. At first, a new capital was created at Samarra (838–83) to house them and keep them away from the population of Baghdad, with whom they had clashed. Eventually they came to wrest effective power from freeborn Muslims all over the Muslim world, acting as kingmakers from the mid-9th century onwards (when they assassinated the caliph al-Mutawakkil and his three successors). They also sapped the Treasury of its funds, further undermining the caliph's rule and causing uncontrollable haemorrhaging of the caliph's resources and authority.

Religiously, as with the *ghulams*, the Abbasid caliphs were the victims of one of their own initiatives. In this case, it was their stress on Muhammad's centrality to Islam in general and to the caliphal office in particular that weakened them. They had justified their overthrow of the Umayyads by highlighting the latter's distance from the Prophet while magnifying their own tenuous connection to him: having an ancestor who was one of Muhammad's uncles is not quite the same as being a linear descendant of the Prophet himself, as disgruntled Shiites pointed out. Still, they were the ones who managed to take charge and that in itself was worth something. The problem with deriving legitimacy and prestige from Muhammad was that in doing so the Abbasid caliphs were elevating the Prophet to a higher status than that enjoyed previously, leaving little room for Abbasid claims to religious authority. Muhammad gave the Abbasids the right to rule, but he also gave the *'ulama'* the right to define orthodoxy, as it was they – rather than the caliphs – who were believed to have preserved an accurate record of his paradigmatic behaviour (*sunna*). The caliphs eventually accepted the status of the *'ulama'*, but not without putting up a fight: al-Ma'mun (r. 813–33) attempted to assert his office's religious authority by subjecting the *'ulama'* to an 'inquisition' (*mihna*), in which the caliph's position on a question of theology was forced on all scholars, with regular investigations into the views of individual *'ulama'*. This *mihna* remained caliphal policy until al-Mutawakkil abandoned it in 848, at which point it was clear that the caliphs had lost both the battle and the war; surprisingly soon thereafter they supported the *'ulama'*, usually through generous patronage.

By the mid-10th century, the Abbasid caliphs had only a vestige of power in Iraq itself. Even there, they were humiliated by the arrival in the capital of the Shiite Buyids, rugged invaders from northern Iran, who revived some Sasanid traditions but kept the Abbasids on the caliphal throne. From this point on, with few exceptions, the Abbasid caliphs were at best spiritual heads of the Islamic world. The Buyids ruled Iraq and western Iran for over a century (945–1055), and were ousted by the Sunni Saljuqs (c. 1037–1157), the first of several waves of Turks to enter the Islamic world voluntarily.

Although all this sounds rather negative – and for the Abbasid caliphs and Iraq more generally it undoubtedly was – 'Islam', as both a religion and civilization, was in very good shape by the end of this period. With the political fragmentation of the caliphate, and the existence of two others based in Cordoba and Cairo, the trappings of Abbasid power and Islamic civilization in general were exported to the various courts that sprung up all over the Islamic world, with truly significant cultural and religious ramifications. The existence of regional centres of Islamic culture, many of which were consciously modelled on the Abbasid court, meant that political energies could be focused on regions that had been too remote to command the caliph's attention in earlier centuries. The spread of Islam beyond its traditional boundaries in the Great Arid Zone was enabled by the actions of regional rulers; the Fatimids and Berbers in North Africa made inroads into sub-Saharan Africa, just as the Ghaznavids did in India, with the sultan Mahmud (r. 997–1030) launching no fewer than 17 raids into the subcontinent. Africa, India, and Southeast

Asia were thus softened up for the large-scale conversion of their populations to Islam that would take place in subsequent centuries.

Crucially, this is also the period in which both Sunnis and Shiites chiselled each other into the mutually distinguishable forms in which they currently exist. The rivalry between the Shiite Buyids and Fatimids on the one hand, and the Sunni Saljuqs and Ghaznavids on the other, had an ideological, sectarian edge to it. Both sides supported *'ulama'*, built libraries and – from the 11th century – law schools (*madrasas*), and dispatched teachers and missionaries throughout Islamic lands and beyond. At its height, the Fatimid caliphate ruled Egypt, North Africa, Sicily, Syria, Yemen, the Hijaz, and parts of East Africa, and Fatimid influence also extended to communities in India. The Shiism they spread was different from that espoused by the Buyids (or, for that matter, by most Shiites in the modern world). All Shiites trace the leadership of the *umma*, the 'imamate', from 'Ali through two of his sons and their descendants. After the death in 765 of the sixth imam, Ja'far, the movement split in two: some followed his son Isma'il (hence, 'Ismailis'), others followed another son, Musa. The latter group continued following the line of imams until, in 874, the twelfth imam (hence, 'Twelvers') disappeared or, as their detractors maintain, died. Under Fatimid patronage, Ismaili Shiism (and under the Buyids, Twelver Shiism) was thoroughly systematized, and the Fatimids challenged their Sunni rivals to the east at all levels. Sunnism's response to the Shiite challenge was impressive: in the 800–1100 period the six most prestigious collections of *hadith*s, or traditions about Muhammad, were assembled; philosophical, theological, and mystical trends in Islam were squared with 'orthodox' Sunnism; and the four schools of Islamic legal thought (*madhhab*s) emerged. By the end of the 11th century, Sunnism is thought finally to have crystallized, with scholars maintaining that from then on the 'gate of interpreting Islamic law' (*ijtihad*) had been closed.

In the 1090s, the gates through which Saljuq and Fatimid power and influence passed had also closed: with the death of the Fatimid caliph in 1094, the Fatimid movement split into two groups, one of which would become known in Europe as the Assassins who set about defeating their enemies not by overwhelming their armies but by picking off their leaders (the movement's name is derived from their suspected use of *hashish* to steady an operative's nerves before he rushed towards near-certain death). One of their first high-profile victims was the Saljuq vizier Nizam al-Mulk, who was the pivot around whom Saljuq power turned. Thereafter, the Fatimids and the Saljuqs of Iran/Iraq declined in tandem. By this time, however, Sunnism and Shiism were set on their respective paths and were less reliant on state patronage than before. Moreover, by the end of this period, Muslims outnumbered non-Muslims in Islamic lands: Islam had thus reached its age of majority in both senses.

1100–1500

The first two periods are often referred to as the 'formative' and 'classical' periods of Islamic history; and for most Muslims (who, it should be noted, tend not to use these terms or chronological divisions), they are the centuries that count the most. But the overwhelming majority of the world's Muslims would almost certainly still be infidels were it not for the events of the 1100–1500 period. And although modern Islamists (those for whom Islam is a political as well as a religious system) shine their spotlight on the age of the Prophet and *Rashidun* caliphs, it is in response to the events of *this* period that Islamist movements emerged. From a European perspective, this is the period without which Turkey would have no case for inclusion into the EU (and no case for being 'Turkey' at all), and without which Russia would have no 'issues' with Muslims to their south. Here is what happened.

Having dominated their neighbours for centuries and dictated the course of their own history, Muslims from the late 11th century onwards often found themselves responding to the actions of others – both Muslims and non-Muslims – who lived beyond Islam's political borders. These outsiders came in three forms: Muslim Turks, non-Muslim invaders (Christians in the west, Mongols in the east), and, finally, Muslim invaders (Timur).

In the second half of the 11th century, waves of Turkish tribes continued to migrate westwards, following the pasturelands on which they depended through northern Iran and into Azerbaijan and Anatolia. From there, they conducted raids (*ghazwa*s, often religiously inspired) into Byzantine territory, provoking a military response. The Turks defeated the Byzantine forces at Manzikert in 1071 and within two decades most of Syria, Palestine, and Anatolia was in their hands. By the 13th century, Anatolia had a substantial population of Muslims and the arrival of successive waves of Turks steadily contributed to the de-Hellenization of the region. Turkish rule in Anatolia was typically decentralized, controlled as it was by competing dynasties only loosely affiliated with the Great Saljuqs in Iran. Their continuous incursions into Byzantine territory led the emperor to seek assistance from western Christians, which brings us to the second form of outsider intervention in Islamic lands.

The Crusades were not merely a response to the Byzantine request for assistance against the Turks; ranging over three continents and five centuries, they were many things to many people. Even the First Crusade, launched in 1095, had less to do with Byzantine–Turkish rivalries than with the wider context of Christian offensives against Islam, and, of course, the recovery of Jerusalem and the Holy Land for Christianity. Muslim historians at the time, to the extent that they were concerned with the Crusades at all (and many of them were not), interpreted them within the context of Christian gains against Muslims in Iberia, Italy, and elsewhere. Sicily, which had been ruled as a Muslim state from the mid-10th century, was re-conquered by a combined force of Normans from Italy and Italian soldiers between 1061 and 1091, though

5. The Islamic world c. 1100

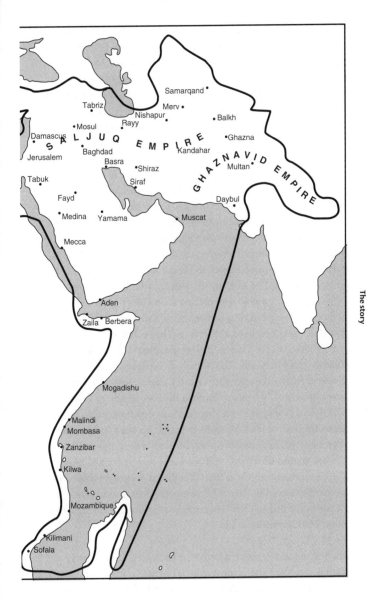

the last Muslims were expelled only in the 1240s. Andalusia was re-conquered more gradually: insofar as local Christians in the north and west of the region forcefully resisted Muslim rule from the 8th century, the *Reconquista* took some 800 years in total, being completed only when Granada fell to Ferdinand and Isabella in 1492. It was only from the late 11th century, however, that Christians had been able to make real progress in the region, with Toledo reverting to Christian rule in 1085.

The *Reconquista* gathered pace and momentum in the 11th century against the backdrop of Muslim political disorganization. Already in 1013 some Berbers sacked Cordoba, and in 1031 the Umayyad caliphate came to an end, its lands fragmenting into minor, regional city-states that fought incessantly against each other. Unable to resist the advance of Christian forces, Muslim rulers appealed for assistance to the Almoravids who ruled in North Africa. The Almoravids were 'puritanical' Berbers, whose early aim was to spread their vision of a rigorous Muslim orthodoxy over what they saw as the superficial and adulterated forms of Islam practised at the time. They ruled in Andalusia from 1086 until 1147, when they were replaced by another Berber dynasty, the Almohads. The Almohads themselves retreated to North Africa by the mid-13th century, when most of Andalusia was lost to the Christians (Cordoba in 1236, Seville in 1248). The dynasty's uncompromising religious doctrines made them fearsome both to local Muslims (who, in this case, had *not* invited them) and to *Reconquista* forces. Most adversely affected were the indigenous Christians and Jews who had flourished under Umayyad rule: with the advent of militant Berber dynasties, they were often forced to choose between conversion, emigration, or death. Some fled to Christian regions of Spain and Portugal or to other Mediterranean lands.

Having to some extent triggered the Crusades, Turks loosely affiliated to the Saljuqs must also be credited with resisting and eventually overcoming them. At the height of their power, the

Great Saljuqs would entrust their provinces to princes of the family who were often too young to rule independently. These princes were thus accompanied by tutor-guardians (*atabeg*s) who would exercise real power – provisionally in theory, permanently in practice. One such *atabeg* was Zangi, ruler of Mosul and Aleppo (r. 1128–46), who managed to inflict the first serious defeat on the Crusaders when he captured Edessa from them in 1146. His son Nur al-Din unified Syria and one of the latter's Kurdish mercenaries conquered Egypt from the Fatimids in 1169. Thereafter, another Sunni Kurd, known to Europeans as Saladin, united Egypt and Syria, putting an end to the Shiite dynasty of the Fatimids in 1171 (thereby achieving his declared goals) and regaining Jerusalem for the Muslims by defeating the Crusaders at Hattin in 1187 (thereby achieving fame).

Saladin's successors in the Ayyubid dynasty that he founded (1174–1250) squabbled continuously, for which they often entered into strategic truces with the Crusaders and surrounded themselves with Turkish slave-soldiers (*mamluk*s) of their own. These Mamluks (r. 1250–1517) overthrew the Ayyubids and ruled a large region that included Egypt, Syria, and parts of Iraq, Arabia, and North and East Africa. Their attachment to the slave-soldier system, which required the regular import of fresh batches of Turks, created a strong and militarily stable society that was able to withstand external challenges. Rather than concluding truces with the Franks (as their predecessors had done), they evicted the Crusaders from Palestine by 1291, having already defeated the Mongols at Ayn Jalut in 1260, victories that effectively put an end to this double-headed threat to Muslims in the Near East.

Muslims elsewhere, however, did not escape the Mongol conquests, and until relatively recently – and certainly at the time – it was the Mongols rather than the Crusaders who commanded the attention of Muslims worldwide. Like the prophet Muhammad, 'Temujin' (r. 1206–27) achieved power by uniting numerous nomadic tribes under his rule, and entered the spotlight at around the age of 40, when he was renamed Chinggis Khan ('supreme ruler'). Moreover, like Muhammad, Chinggis did not live to see his state expand into a world empire; by the time he died, the Mongols had conquered a large part of Central Asia, but had yet to incorporate those parts of China, Korea, Eastern Europe, the Caucasus, and the Islamic world that eventually would comprise the Mongol empire. Substantial parts of Muslim Central Asia and northern Iran were conquered early on, with devastating consequences – accounts of Mongol destruction are chilling even when filtered for hyperbole. Most devastating to Muslims was the Mongol conquest of Iran/Iraq in the 1250s: the fragile irrigation system that sustained Iraq's agriculture was destroyed, as were libraries, mosques, and entire populations in leading towns and cities. But what looms largest in Muslim memory is the sacking of Baghdad in 1258, which put an end to the Abbasid caliphate after 500 years of existence. The Mongol rulers of Iran/Iraq (the 'Ilkhans', r. 1265–1335) eventually converted to Islam and attempted to curry the favour of local Muslims by patronizing arts, employing Persian administrators, and decreasing taxation. But then as now, for their part in unplugging the Abbasids' life-support machine, the Mongols were seen as villains.

The Mamluks, on the other hand, emerged as the heroes. The logic behind using Turkish slaves in early Abbasid times was that they were barred by their slave status from laying claim to the caliphal office. Though they did not claim to be caliphs, their servile background remained an issue for the Mamluk sultans, for which purpose they presented themselves as champions of *jihad* against infidels, and imported an uncle of the last Abbasid caliph to Egypt, where his presence lent legitimacy to Mamluk rule. The sultans also patronized *'ulama'* and supported a host of religious foundations and building projects. Scholars on their payroll wrote our history books and generally said nice things about them. But even the Mamluks, defenders of Islam against the Mongols and the Crusaders, were unable to resist the Black Death of the 1340s, which they inadvertently helped to spread and from which they never quite recovered.

Politically, towards the end of this period, the central Islamic lands were in disarray. Not only were the Mamluks in decline, but from Transoxania in the northeast a devastating campaign by the Turco-Mongol ruler Timur ('Tamerlane', 1336–1405) was unleashed along the lines of the earlier Mongol conquests. Timur's religion was Islam but his culture and identity were self-consciously Mongol (even the Islam that he and his followers practised was permeated by Mongol traditions), and he seems to have targeted only those lands that Chinggis and his successors had conquered. Although he defeated Muslim armies in Delhi (1398), Aleppo (1400), Damascus (1401), Anatolia (1402), and elsewhere, he created no lasting empire. Upon his death in 1405, his lands were divided amongst four sons, none of whom was as militarily ambitious as their father.

Timur's conquests do serve to highlight the strengths and weaknesses of the various Muslim polities in the early 15th century. It is telling that he gained far more booty from his conquests in Muslim India than anywhere else, and it is in India and neighbouring regions that Islamic rule and religion would make impressive progress in this period. India had been targeted systematically by Muslim rulers since Ghaznavid times, but it is only from the late 12th and early 13th centuries that Muslims would rule there independently, first under the Ghurids from Afghanistan (r. 1148–1218), and then under Turkish and Afghani dynasties that comprised the Delhi Sultanate (1206–1526). As often in Islamic history, a slave-soldier of one dynasty broke away from his masters and created a dynasty of his own. In this case, it was Aybeg, a *ghulam* of the Ghurids, who conquered Delhi in 1206 and established a *mamluk* state in India. Although he died five years later in a freak polo accident, one of his own *ghulam*s succeeded him, creating a dynasty of slave-soldiers that would last until 1290. For the next two centuries a specifically

Indo-Muslim culture was created in the region, and Islam spread in the subcontinent and beyond, to what are now Malaysia and Indonesia.

Though the Mongols and Timur spread destruction across the Islamic lands, their conquests also led to the spread of everything from Persian literature to playing cards. The crucial point is that the decline and fall of the Abbasid caliphate, and of political structures and institutions more generally, were paralleled by (and related to) the creation of alternative social and political structures within Muslim societies, most significantly, Sufi organizations. Sufism, as a mystical approach to God, is in some ways as old as Islam itself, though it was only in the 9th century that its formal doctrines emerged, and only from the 13th that specific branches of Sufism became institutionalized. These 'brotherhoods' (*tariqas*), with their 'lodges' (*khanqas*, *ribats*, or *zawiyas*, depending on the region), 'masters' (*shaykhs* or *pirs*, among other terms), initiation ceremonies, and unusual rituals, might conjure up for Westerners images of Freemasonry, with spirituality rather than stonecutting as their basis. But unlike Freemasonry, Sufism did have real social, political, and religious influence, and it is largely to the efforts of charismatic Sufi leaders that large parts of sub-Saharan Africa, South and Southeast Asia owe their introduction to Islam.

Islam first won over converts amongst peoples in the Near East who were closely familiar with Semitic monotheism: it is a short distance from Aramaic to Arabic and from 'Abraham' to 'Ibrahim'. Judaism and Christianity's relationship with Islam was so close that the doctrine emerged in Islam that Judaism and Christianity *were* originally Islam itself but that the religion had been corrupted over time, for which purpose God had to remind mankind of the True Path by sending it Muhammad and the Quran. Such a doctrine could not reasonably be extended to include Hinduism, Buddhism, or the pagan religions of Africa and Southeast Asia, but Sufi leaders proved otherwise. In a nutshell,

Sufi missionaries convinced pagans and polytheists that they were essentially *already* Muslims, but that their deities and rituals went by different names in the language of Islam. For this approach to work, however, only a very superficial version of Islam could be propagated, and elements of the pre-Islamic religions that had no equivalent in Islam had to be accommodated into the converts' new religion (just as St Valentine's Day, Halloween, and Christmas trees found their way into Christian cultures). This happened seamlessly amongst monotheistic converts – retellings of Bible stories, known as *Isra'iliyyat*, seeped into the Islamic tradition, often undetected. In the cases of pagans and polytheists, however, the result was a religious syncretism that was deeply offensive to 'orthodox' Muslims. We have encountered an early case of this in the Almoravid response to Berber Islam, and most modern Islamist movements have their origins in similar attempts to cleanse Muslim societies of syncretistic and otherwise adulterated forms of belief and worship.

In the 14th and 15th centuries, Sufi movements were active and influential amongst Turks in Anatolia and Azerbaijan (and in most other regions, for that matter). The various elements of Sunni, Shiite, heterodox Sufi, and other ideas that were braided together in this region, were gradually disentangled in the late 15th and early 16th centuries, to produce the Sunni Ottomans and the Shiite Safavids, whose empires' legacies and descendants have combined to create the modern Near East.

1500 to present

When does Islamic history end? Although in some parts of the world its end is nowhere in sight, there are three important ways in which Islamic history can be said to have ended in the '1500 to present' period. First, as will be seen in Chapters 6 and 7, those episodes of history that make up the historical repository common to all Muslims belong to the three periods already described. Second, in this period the history that concerns Islam and

6. The Islamic world c. 1700

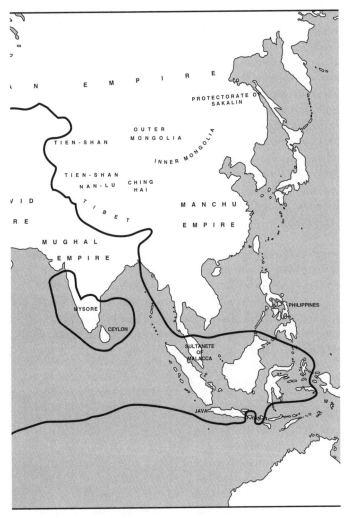

Within the map: N EMPIRE, PROTECTORATE OF SAKALIN, TIEN-SHAN, OUTER MONGOLIA, INNER MONGOLIA, TIEN-SHAN NAN-LU, CHING HAI, TIBET, MANCHU EMPIRE, VID RE, MUGHAL EMPIRE, MYSORE, CEYLON, PHILIPPINES, SULTANETE OF MALACCA, JAVA

Muslims is less 'Islamic' history than it is 'World' history in which Islam and Muslims play a role. As this role is often secondary, deeming events in this period to be part of 'Islamic' history lends Islam and Muslims a measure of control over developments that is at best misleading. Thus, when the French occupied Egypt in 1798 it was the British who kicked them out; the Egyptians themselves could only watch from the sidelines. Third, this is the period that witnessed the erosion of many salient features of pre-modern Muslim societies and of Islamic history, including the widespread reliance on slave-soldiers (and cavalry more generally), the legal distinction between Muslims and others in Islamic lands, the centrality of the *hajj* (and other religious networks) to the *umma*'s cohesion, and the *'ulama*'s control over religious authority, among other things.

For all that, a large proportion of today's Muslims are descendants of those who converted in this period, and 'in the sixteenth century of our era, a visitor from Mars might have supposed that the human world was on the verge of becoming Muslim', as one historian put it. Our Martian guest would have been led to this conclusion by the contemporaneous existence of great Muslim empires and civilizations created by the Ottomans (1300–1922), Safavids (1501–1722), and Mughals (1526–1858). Here is a [human] view of what it looked like.

The Ottoman empire was the first Muslim super-state of this period to rise and the last to fall, lasting in some form or another from the early 14th to the early 20th centuries. It rose when, in c. 1300, an ambitious leader of Turkish frontier warriors in western Anatolia managed to carve out an independent Muslim state in the region. The state, named after its founder Osman (in a garbled European pronunciation, 'Ottoman'), expanded rapidly at the expense of the Byzantine empire, and in 1453 the Ottomans conquered Constantinople (in a garbled Turkish pronunciation, 'Istanbul'). Over the following century, they would take Jerusalem, Mecca, and Medina from the Mamluk Sultanate (which they conquered in 1517) and Baghdad from the Safavids in 1534, while expanding westwards into Europe, adding Belgrade and Hungary to their realms, and besieging Vienna in 1529. The Ottoman sultans were quick to capitalize on their gains to obtain power, wealth, and prestige: money, libraries, archives, and *'ulama'* were imported to Istanbul from the newly conquered territories of Egypt and Syria, and the sultans claimed to inherit the authority – as well as the lands – of conquered rulers, calling themselves 'Caesar', 'Shahanshah', and 'Caliph' – even, on occasion, 'God's Caliph'. Unsurprisingly, the sultans or 'caliphs' assumed religious roles, issuing religious edicts, appointing *qadi*s, and integrating the *'ulama'* into the ruling hierarchy. For his military successes in this period, the sultan Sulayman (r. 1520–66) was known to Europeans as 'the Magnificent'; for his integration of customary law into the *shari'a*, he was known to Muslims as 'the Lawgiver'.

By the mid-16th century, the Ottomans had created a strong, centralized, and cosmopolitan empire that incorporated some of Islam's – and the world's – greatest cities and resources, with footholds in Europe, Asia, and Africa. But being cosmopolitan proved to have both positive and negative results: on the one hand, trade and culture in Ottoman cities were boosted through the absorption of tens of thousands of Jewish refugees from the Spanish Inquisition; the Ottoman military machine was partly made up of Christian youths ('Janissaries', or 'new soldiers', in Turkish); and, having inherited the disparate groups of Turkmen who inhabited Anatolia between the 13th and 15th centuries, the Ottomans ruled over a significant population of Shiites and Sufis (sometimes possessing radically unorthodox beliefs), as well as various groups of Christians. The ethnic composition of the empire was no less varied. On the other hand, by the end of the 19th century, it would be clear that there was very little to unite this patchwork of populations. Moreover, though it was all well and good to assume religious titles, control the *'ulama'*, and take pride in one's authority over holy cities, the fact is that even at its height, barely half of the empire's subjects were Muslims, and less than half of the world's Muslims were Ottomans. Unification of the *umma* such as that achieved (if only politically) by the early caliphs would have been worth far more for a Muslim ruler than political control over Albania and Croatia. Furthermore, developments that held real significance to Islam and Muslims were also happening elsewhere, in Safavid and Mughal lands.

Around the time that Osman was creating his state in Anatolia, a native of Azerbaijan named Safi al-Din (1252–1334) founded a Sufi brotherhood in Ardabil, whose followers came to be known as Safavids. By the late 15th century, this brotherhood had morphed into a militant Shiite–Sufi movement that held its leader to be either the hidden Imam or God Himself. At the turn of the 16th century, the leader of the Safavid order, a teenager named Isma'il, came out of hiding and set about conquering Iran; by 1501, he was the region's shah with a capital at Tabriz. In 1514, however, the Safavid forces were defeated by the Ottomans at Chaldiran, with three significant consequences: first, the modern Turkish–Iranian border was set; second, having lost the battle (and their claim to divinity) to Ottoman gunpowder, the Safavid shahs acquired gunpowder too; and third, with Ottoman forces encroaching on their western provinces, subsequent shahs moved the capital eastwards, eventually settling on Isfahan under 'Abbas I (r. 1587–1629).

In moving eastwards, the Safavids were distancing themselves from their original Turkmen power-base, and digging their heels into Iran's heartland. The religious character of the state was purged of its radical ideas, which were replaced with orthodox, Twelver Shiism (while Turkish elites were replaced with Persian ones). This form of Shiism was forcibly imposed on a largely Sunni population, and Shiite scholars from Bahrain, Greater Syria, and Iraq were imported to Isfahan, where both religious and secular culture flourished. To his capital in Isfahan, 'Abbas also shifted populations from provincial towns to create a cultural and economic hub. It was thus under the Safavids that

Iran's modern borders and religious and cultural identities were brought into clear focus – in sharp contrast to the tolerant heterogeneity of the Ottoman empire. Persian literature reached new heights and, to the extent that both the Ottomans and Mughals (or 'Moghuls', Persian for 'Mongols') had adopted Persian as the language of high culture (in pre-Ottoman Anatolia and pre-Mughal India), the Safavids were at the very centre of Islamic civilization. After the death of 'Abbas II (r. 1642–66), however, decline set in: natural disasters (famines, earthquakes, and the spread of diseases) combined with ineffectual rulers to leave a political vacuum that was filled by Shiite *'ulama'*, or 'mullahs', who tightened Shiism's hold on society. Imposing one's religion by force is no way to win friends and influence people, and embittered Sunni tribesmen from Afghanistan overran the Safavids in 1722, putting an end to their rule. Political unity – and Shiism – returned to Iran with the Qajars (1794–1925), who ushered Iran into modernity.

From elsewhere in Afghanistan in the early 16th century, a prince known as Babur launched a successful raid into India. As Babur had claimed descent from both Chinggis Khan and Timur, it was a safe bet that he would try to conquer *something*. This he did in 1526, when his forces defeated the sultan of Delhi and established a dynasty in India. It was under his grandson Akbar (r. 1556–1605), however, that the Mughal empire was created, and for the next century and half Akbar and his successors flourished and their territories expanded. By the reign of Aurangzeb (1658–1707), the Mughals ruled almost all of the Indian subcontinent, as well as parts of Iran and Central Asia, with a combined population of some 100 million people. Though the overwhelming majority of these subjects were not Muslims, they were fully integrated into society at all levels, enjoying unprecedented tolerance: they were exempt from paying the *jizya* poll-tax, Mughal emperors married Hindu wives, and the Muslim lunar calendar was abandoned by Akbar in favour of a solar one. Mughal culture fused Islamic traditions with Indian ones, creating new forms and setting new standards in painting, poetry, and architecture. The legacy of their achievements can be seen today in the magnificence of the Taj Mahal and in the use of the term 'mogul' with reference to those who possess power and wealth.

Not all of Akbar's ideas were readily adopted by his successors, however. In 1581, Akbar founded what he called the *Din-i Ilahi*, or 'Divine Religion', which aimed to accommodate the many truths of all religions known to him within a single system. Even Sufi missionaries could not get away with such a scheme and the most vocal opposition to this heresy came from the Sufi leader Ahmad Sirhindi (1564–1624). Akbar's experiment did not survive his death and eventually the excesses of tolerance offered to non-Muslims triggered excesses of intolerance: Aurangzeb waged *jihad* against Hindus, with mixed results. The empire's borders reached their greatest extent, but with more land to rule and fewer locals willing to cooperate, the Mughals declined rapidly, losing effective power from as early as 1725 (though the state would survive until 1857). In 1803, with the region parcelled out among local Hindu and British rulers, a leader of the *'ulama'* in Delhi declared that India was no longer a Muslim country.

But what were the British – and other Europeans – doing in Asia at all? The quick answer, then as now, is 'buying things'. From the 16th century, small nations with big ships (the Dutch and the Portuguese) and later big nations with big ships (the British and French) sought to gain control over trade routes to the Far East, from which spices and other commodities could be bought directly (and hence cheaply). For centuries, Muslim states and societies had benefited from their strategic location, serving as a bridge between Europe and Asia. In the pre-modern period, the geographical centrality of the Muslim world was combined with its superior culture, political organization, and military strength, which allowed Muslims to dominate much of Afro-Eurasia at a time when Europeans were – in relative terms – only beginning to climb down from the trees. But in the 17th and, especially, 18th centuries, the decline of the great Muslim empires coincided with the rise of European ones.

As a result of the Industrial Revolution, Europeans gained important production and communication advantages; the Napoleonic Wars (1793–1815) channelled industrial efforts towards military objectives; the French Revolution mobilized large sectors of the population by encouraging patriotism and notions of state service; and the Enlightenment generated scientific justification for the existence of a hierarchy of civilizations (at the top of which were Europeans, of course). As the three great Muslim empires were largely land-based, they would have been unable to compete with European ships, even had they been at the height of their strength, which they were not. The Mughals and Safavids lost power in the early 18th century, and the Ottomans managed to survive only by reorganizing their empire along European lines. The failed Ottoman siege of Vienna in 1683, and the humiliating defeats suffered in the Russian–Ottoman war of 1768–74 disabused the sultans of any ideas that they were militarily superior – or even equal – to European powers. Decentralization of the empire, factionalism within the court, and other internal instabilities contributed to the impression that the Ottoman empire was 'the sick man of Europe'. In response, from the time of Selim III (r. 1789–1807) sultans sought to reassert themselves through internal measures, leading to the 'reorganization' (*Tanzimat*) of the empire (c. 1839–76), through which secular law replaced *shari'a*, non-Muslims were made equal to Muslims, and Ottoman administration was modernized in most respects. The autocrat (or, as he saw it, 'caliph') 'Abdul Hamid II (r. 1876–1909) introduced a rail network to the [shrinking] empire, and invested heavily in building projects. Tellingly, whereas previous sultans proudly sponsored the creation of mosques and other religious buildings, 'Abdul Hamid's projects were almost exclusively secular. Large-scale modernization was expensive, for which reason Muslim states found themselves owing large sums to European ones;

and Europeans soon found themselves in political control of Muslim lands.

None of this was inevitable, however, and in some parts of the Muslim world things went in an entirely different direction. In the 16th century, Bedouin from the Sahara moved north to take control of the Moroccan heartland, creating a dynasty of *sharif*s (those claiming lineal descent from the Prophet) who ruled from Marrakech; Sharifian dynasties have ruled over Morocco ever since. The Sa'adi dynasty (r. 1554–1659) managed to cross what was once thought to be a militarily impenetrable Sahara, destroying the Songhay state in West Africa and its legendary capital, Timbuktu, in 1591. They also repelled Spanish and Portuguese forces in 1578, and withstood Ottoman challenges, partly by playing the British and Spanish off each other, all of which enabled them to remain an independent Muslim state. Sharifian states managed to stave off Europeans until the late 19th century and the Alaouite Sharifian dynasty (r. 1666 to present) was the first state to recognize the newly independent United States of America. Even they, however, eventually succumbed to colonialism: in 1912, the French established a protectorate in Morocco, from which the Moroccans gained independence under Muhammad V (r. 1927–61) in 1956.

Most Muslim societies had experienced foreign rule over the preceding millennium when Turks, Mongols, Berbers, and – in some periods and regions – Arabs ruled as outsiders, often with little sensitivity to local traditions and concerns. What made European colonialism particularly unpopular were three things. First, like the Crusaders, colonial powers were non-Muslim, and were often in direct competition with Muslims to spread their faith (a competition that Muslims usually won). Unlike the Crusaders, however, they were ever-present and of relevance to nearly all Muslims. Second, Muslim societies in this period became aware of mechanisms for resisting colonialism and alternatives to it, aside from the *jihad* that some espoused.

Pan-Islamism, Pan-Arabism, and Pan-Turkism followed the lead of national liberation movements elsewhere, thereby raising Muslim expectations of overcoming foreign rule and influence. Third, with the spread of modern communications and media, the realities of the preceding points were broadcast far and wide.

From the 19th century (and, to a degree, much earlier), various movements aimed at reasserting and purifying 'Islam' emerged in different parts of the Muslim world, targeting both external forces (colonialism) and internal ones (supposedly superficial or syncretistic practice of Islam, and the secularization of Muslim societies and their rulers). Although individual movements were often identified with a particular grievance, in time many of these groups – and most of their followers – came either to conflate a variety of battle-cries or to dissolve specific complaints into a general feeling that 'things are not as they should be', to which the solution was change along uncompromising Islamic lines. What was particularly galling to them was that the Muslim leadership was seen to contribute to the problem rather than to its solution. These thinkers and activists tended to call themselves *mujaddid*s, or 'renovators'; we tend to call them 'Islamists' (a term that encompasses many other groups too). Though its roots are often traced back to Muhammad ibn 'Abd al-Wahhab (d. 1787), Islamism itself was transformed in the 20th century, with the establishment of Hasan al-Banna's (d. 1949) Muslim Brotherhood (Egypt, 1928) and Abu l-'Ala Mawdudi's (d. 1979) *Jama'at-i Islami*, or 'Islamic Society' (India, 1941). The former targeted foreign colonialists and indigenous secularists, while the latter focused on the British and their Hindu allies. These movements were quickly internationalized, spawning numerous offshoots: Mawdudi's ideas influenced the prominent Egyptian Islamist Sayyid Qutb (d. 1966), who himself belonged to the Muslim Brotherhood (members of which created Hamas in 1987).

Though the key to understanding Muslim societies in the 19th century is said to be colonialism, an underrated factor of great significance is the spread of printing throughout Muslim lands in this period. Printing led, amongst other things, to the spread of newspapers, with governmental journals established in Egypt (1824), Turkey and other Ottoman provinces (1831), Iran (1837), and elsewhere in subsequent years. Crucially, the leading Islamic reformists edited newspapers and disseminated their ideas through them. Ideologues such as Muhammad 'Abduh (d. 1906) and Jamal al-Din al-Afghani (d. 1897) published a free religious newspaper in which Islamist and anti-British ideas were voiced, reaching readers throughout the Muslim world (except in Egypt and India, where the British banned it). 'Abduh's disciple Rashid Rida (d. 1935) edited the Islamic magazine *al-Manar* for almost 40 years, through which his teacher's ideas were circulated widely, alongside his own proposals for the creation of a Pan-Islamic caliphate.

What printing also accomplished, albeit inadvertently, is the democratization of religious authority. In the past, Islamic teachings were propagated through personal interactions with *'ulama'* or Sufi leaders. Only those respected leaders who were able, by virtue of their religious learning and reputation, to attract a following could wield influence. With the spread of modern media (starting, but not ending, with printing) anyone with access to the requisite technology could influence millions of people. Religious credentials and local reputation were no longer as important as the medium of communication. This development often disturbed the fine balance achieved between the *'ulama'* and political authorities, a balance that had been maintained by controlling the *'ulama'* or supporting the compliant members within their ranks, at the expense of popular Sufi orders. The matrix was thus complicated by the rise of Islamists who had little time for most Sufis and for Westernized Muslim politicians (or the *'ulama'* who were deemed to have sold out to them).

What all this demonstrates, of course, is that it is simplistic to view Islamism as a reactive rejection of 'the West' and its ways. Islamists have been happy to acquire and use both the hardware and the software of modern, Western civilization in furthering their cause. Ayatollah Khomeini famously propagated his revolutionary message through audio cassettes, and al-Qaeda makes full use of communications technology, releasing messages to media outlets, communicating via internet chat-rooms, and exploiting for recruitment purposes the media attention that erupts around their operations. Martyrdom messages and gruesome beheadings on video-sharing websites are further examples of this willingness to benefit from such technologies. In terms of software, Western ideas have been appropriated even by those seeking liberation from Western influence: although Pan-Islamism might be said to have pre-modern roots, national liberation movements, from Chechnya to Palestine and Xinjiang, are Western imports. Similarly, the anti-Semitic theories that are widely espoused by Muslims aiming to reverse the effects of colonialism and imperialism (for which, according to these theories, the Jews are responsible), are themselves Western, imperialist products – Muslim societies had nothing like them until [Christian] Arabs imported the ideas from Europe to Muslim lands in the 19th century. For their part, the overwhelming majority of Muslims, who reject Islamist ideologies, are also increasingly embracing modern technologies and Western ideas, with interesting results: some have [convincingly] demonstrated the Muslim role in the rise of modern science, medicine, and technology; others have [less convincingly] attempted to show that such 'Western' ideas as democracy, human rights, and egalitarianism are ultimately traceable to early Islam. Although this might suggest that Muslims are becoming increasingly Westernized, it also shows how easily Westernization can be adapted to Islam.

Conclusion

So that, in the broadest of strokes, is what happened. As is to be expected from any survey of 1,400 years of history, spanning three continents, we have encountered our fair share of rulers, battles, dates, and similar-sounding names. I have tried to balance these with a sense of how Islam itself developed in each period and will limit myself here to a single conclusion that relates to both the political and religious developments covered above.

Once an empire was established following the early Islamic conquests, the spread of Islam as a religion, on the one hand, and as a political power, on the other, did not always overlap: in many cases, in fact, Islam did particularly well when Muslim rulers were doing particularly poorly. Thus, Islam gained more converts during the period of European colonial rule than in any other period, and in the post-colonial period the geographical distribution of Muslims was also dramatically increased: without the British in India and the French in North Africa, there would be few Pakistanis in Britain and few Algerians in France. And although the Deobandi movement began as a reaction to British rule in India, a missionary offshoot of the movement now controls almost half of the mosques in the United Kingdom, accounts for more than three-quarters of domestically trained Muslim clerics, and plans to create Europe's largest mosque next to the site of the 2012 Olympics in London. An interesting ramification of this is that – assuming historical trends persist – even if attempts to establish a worldwide caliphate succeed, they will not necessarily be accompanied by a corresponding spread of Islam itself. In fact, if demographic and statistical trends persist, before too long – even without a caliphate – a third of humanity might well be Muslim.

Chapter 2
Peoples and cultures

Much of the story of Islamic history, as recounted above, is dominated by the same factors that shape the histories of other societies, namely geographical realities and the spread of technologies – from camels to cars, and from papyrus and parchment to paper and then printing. The *hajj*, for instance, has evolved from being a ritual dependent upon caravans to an enterprise serviced by aeroplanes. And although modern technology has enabled unprecedented numbers of Muslims to perform the pilgrimage to Mecca, it has also decreased the *hajj*'s role as a means for spreading ideas, commodities, news, and the sense of a unified *umma*. It may be interesting to see how 'neutral' developments have affected 'Islamic' institutions such as the *hajj*, but this in itself does not constitute a particularly 'Islamic' history; it is merely world history through Islamic examples. What *is* particular to Islamic history are those peoples – the Arabs, Persians, and Turks – who created it, by guiding geography and technology (amongst other factors) in very particular directions.

The Arabs

In 2003, Robert Kilroy-Silk, a British media personality and politician, wrote an article in *The Sunday Express* entitled 'We owe Arabs nothing', in which he stated that Arabs are little more than 'suicide bombers, limb-amputators, [and] women-repressors'. Condemnation of the article and its author was predictably swift, with the Muslim Council of Britain leading the protests. That objectionable ideas should trigger objections is never surprising. What is surprising in this case is that objection to an article about *Arabs* was led by *non-Arab* Muslims. Although it is widely known that most Muslims are not Arabs, it is clear that Arabs have played so central a role in Islamic history and civilization that 'Arabs' and 'Muslims' are regularly conflated by Islam's supporters and detractors alike.

Interestingly, from the vantage-point of very early Islamic history, the conflation is not entirely unreasonable. It could be argued that Islam began as a chosen-people religion aimed exclusively at the Arabs; the Quran (12: 2, and 43: 3) states that it is in the Arabic language 'so that you may understand [its message]', a statement that assumes its audience to be Arabic-speakers. Moreover, under the Umayyad caliphs, the conversion of non-Arabs to Islam was normally discouraged and those who *did* convert were made 'clients' of Arab tribes. In other words, to be a Muslim one had to be an Arab – or at least an honorary one. And for centuries, Jews in Muslim lands (usually in Persia) argued that Muhammad was indeed a true Prophet sent by God to spread monotheism, but only amongst the pagan Arabs who needed it. (Persian Jews no longer subscribe to this theory.) Support for such an idea comes from the Quran itself (46: 12), which states: 'And before this, was the Book of Moses as a guide and a mercy: And this Book confirms (it) in the Arabic tongue...'

Clearly, however, that is not the only way of looking at things and is certainly not how things turned out. Still, the Arabs and their culture have been central to all Muslims in a number of ways. The early association of Islam with Arabs, together with the long-standing objection (now obsolete) to translating the Quran, have meant that even non-Arab Muslims have had reason to learn at least the basics of Arabic. And it does no harm that

Arabic is regarded – even amongst Persians – as the language of God (though most Muslim historians hold that Adam and Eve spoke Aramaic). Crucially, those who want to read the seminal works of Islamic law, theology, Quranic studies, *hadith*, history, and so forth must have a thorough grounding in Arabic. As Islam spread for the most part in regions and periods where literacy was very limited, a Muslim's first experience of literacy often involved learning to read and write God's language.

Consequently, even non-Arabic languages came to be written in a version of the Arabic script modified to accommodate the particularities of the spoken languages. Persian, Urdu (Hindi in Arabic script), and – until relatively recently – Turkish, as well as a host of other languages, use the Arabic alphabet and contain numerous Arabic words. For these reasons, in the first few centuries of Islamic history all authors regardless of ethnicity would compose their works in Arabic. Arabic might thus be compared with Chinese, the stability of which over millennia allowed Chinese scholars to read about and build on their predecessors' ideas, with the result that many world-changing inventions originated there – from paper, printing, the compass, and gunpowder, to magic tricks and kung-fu. As a scholarly language shared by non-native speakers, Arabic also brings to mind the use of Latin in pre- and early-modern Europe. The spread of Arabic as a scholarly language allowed scholars, Muslim and non-Muslim alike, to communicate their ideas across boundaries and generations, with truly impressive results in many fields. In the 9th century, for instance, a considerable portion of the ancient Greek writings was translated into Arabic under caliphal auspices, at a time when most in the West had lost the ability to enjoy this heritage, and it is through translations into Latin of these Arabic versions of Greek texts that Europe rediscovered many of these works and their ideas. Thus, it has been argued (if not widely accepted) that the Renaissance as we know it would not have happened had the Arabs and their language remained in Arabia.

Of course, the creation of an Islamic civilization would not have happened had the Arabs remained in Arabia, and it is they who conquered the Near East, North Africa, Iberia, and Central Asia. Moreover, Arabs provided the political and ideological foundations on which the Umayyad and Abbasid empires were built. But whereas Arabic and its culture have maintained their importance for Islam into modern times, the Arabs themselves have in some ways been left behind: even at the height of Arabo-Islamic culture in the 9th and 10th centuries, most cultural luminaries were non-Arabs. Al-Kindi (d. 873) was known as 'the philosopher of the Arabs' not because most philosophers were Arabs but precisely because they were not. From the 10th century onwards, Arabs have often found themselves under the rule of others – usually Persian, Berber, or Turkish coreligionists.

In the aftermath of the First World War, the break-up of the Ottoman empire witnessed a general reconfiguration of the Near East's ethnic and religious elements, with different groups scrambling to create national and supra-national identities. Although the search for communal identity started with Islam, which provided a ready-made unifier with its idea of the *umma*, many Arab intellectuals were Christians and they sought to promote 'Arab' rather than 'Islamic' identity. Thus, Arab Nationalism and Pan-Arabism were consciously secular (often socialist) movements. Owing to the failure of Nasser's Pan-Arab experiment (1958–61), the inability of Arab states to defeat Israel, and much more besides, Islamic ideologies have once again risen to replace Arab unity as the unifying element in the Near East and beyond.

In this context, the boundaries between Arabo-centric and Islamo-centric movements have sometimes been blurred: Michel Aflaq (d. 1989), a leading Arab Nationalist, made the case that the Arabs' greatest achievement was Islam and its greatest hero Muhammad; this despite the fact that Aflaq was a Syrian Christian. Furthermore, individuals and entire nations have managed simultaneously to cultivate multiple identities:

Muammar Qaddafi has championed both African and Arab unity; some Lebanese have been exploring their Phoenician roots and Palestinians their Canaanite background, to name but a few examples. Interestingly, although 'Islam' and the 'Arabs' initially were inseparable – to be a Muslim one *had* to be an Arab – by the mid-20th-century, Arab ideologies and Islamic ones were in direct competition for the hearts and minds of Near Eastern peoples. In the Arab world Islamic movements have gained the ascendancy, but to its east, in Iran, the competition between religious and ethnic allegiances is a more closely run contest.

The Persians

The Arabs and, as we will see, Turks owe their prominence on the world stage to Islam. The Persians do not. Persians have a proud and long history of statehood that dates back to the Achaemenid period (559–330 BCE); when Arab conquerors defeated the Sasanid empire (224–651), they were putting an end to some 12 centuries of almost uninterrupted Persian self-rule and political autonomy. Thus, whereas the rise of Islam was an unmitigated success for the Arabs and Turks, it was something of a mixed blessing for the Persians, who gained monotheism and the True Religion, but lost their empire and independence. And although the early Muslims created their state in formerly Byzantine and Sasanid lands, the Sasanids paid the higher price of the two: conquered Byzantine subjects could flee to parts of the empire that had not been conquered and any Christian, Greek culture that had been uprooted by the conquests could be replanted in surviving Byzantine lands. The whole of the Sasanid empire, however, was conquered by Muslims, and although some Zoroastrians did flee to India (where they have been known as 'Parsees' ever since), Persian culture had nowhere to go but underground. All of this had short-term, medium-term, and long-term consequences.

In the short term, the Persian people (and landscape) resisted the Arab armies fiercely, which meant that in some provinces caliphal rule, conversion to Islam, Arab settlement, and Arabization were superficial. In most regions, Persian notables were allowed to retain a measure of power and Persian administrative traditions endured accordingly. Curiously, many Persians viewed the Muslim conquests as a temporary, reversible blip, and for the next two centuries an array of 'redeemers' appeared with the declared aim of restoring the pre-Islamic political, social, and religious status quo. Some modern historians and even some observers at the time have (wrongly) viewed various events in Islamic history as examples of Persian-redemption movements, including the Abbasid Revolution, the creation of Baghdad, the rise of the Buyids, Samanids, and Safavids, and the adoption by the Safavid rulers and their subjects of Shiism. Such an interpretation of events is incorrect in each case, but it is accurate in its general awareness of the traumatic impact that the rise of Islam had on many Persians.

In the medium term, rather than attempting to reverse the effects of Islam's arrival, Persians and Persian culture were Islamicized. This happened most obviously under the Abbasids who, by moving to Iraq, constructed their power-base from the rubble of Sasanid institutions. Not only was political and governmental organization inherited from Persian traditions (as Byzantine ones had been inherited by the Umayyads in Syria), but much of Abbasid civilization – including literature, history, theology, religious sciences, Quranic studies, and even Arabic poetry and linguistics – was created and dominated by people who composed books in Arabic but told bedtime stories in Persian. Persians were very much aware of their cultural dominance and a literary movement arose promoting Persian culture and reminding the Arabs of their indebtedness to it. Even the great Ibn Khaldun (d. 1406), writing in the far west of the Islamic world, included in his *Muqaddima* (on which, see below p. 105) a section entitled 'Most of the scholars of Islam have been Persians (*'ajam*)'.

In the long term, Islamic culture itself was Persianized, even in the face of viable alternatives. This process began with the rise of semi-independent Persian dynasties in the Abbasid east, where rulers adopted Sasanid titles, traced for their dynasties Sasanid genealogies, and, most importantly, patronized literature in the Persian language. Perhaps the most famous literary work in Persian, the *Shahnama* ('Book of Kings'), was composed in Samanid times and dedicated to a Ghaznavid ruler. It recounts in epic form all of Iranian history that is thought to have really mattered, beginning with the creation of the world and, tellingly, ending abruptly with the Muslim defeat of the Sasanid forces at the Battle of al-Qadisiyya (637).

Above all, the spread of Turks, Mongols, and Turco-Mongols to and within Islamic lands led to an efflorescence of Persian literature, even – or especially – outside of Iran. Persian-speaking missionaries played a pivotal role in the spread of Islam to the east, and it is no coincidence that the religious terminology used by Chinese Muslims prefers Persian words such as *namaz* ('prayer') over Arabic synonyms (in this case, *salat*). Before entering the Islamic world in the late 10th century, the Turkish tribes from whom the Saljuqs and Ottomans are descended were converted to Islam by Persians; religion was thus filtered to them through a Persian sieve. When the Saljuqs created a dynasty in Iran/Iraq, its administrative and literary forms were Persian, and when their relatives moved westwards to conquer Anatolia and create the Ottoman empire, here too Persian was adopted as the language of culture.

The Mongol and Timurid conquests, destructive though they were, also contributed to the success of the Persian language: on the one hand, having no attachment to Arabic as a religious language, the Mongols in Iran (who employed local, Iranian administrators) patronized Persian scholarship even in those fields that hitherto had been reserved for Arabic. On the other hand, the havoc wrought by the conquests forced leading Iranian scholars to seek safety (and patronage) elsewhere, mostly in Muslim India. Under the Delhi and, especially, the Mughal sultans Indo-Islamic literature, the arts (painting, in particular), and imperial administration were Persian in language and form, and some of the finest specimens of Persian culture were produced in Mughal lands. Thus, from the 11th to 19th centuries (even later, in some regions) Persian was the leading language of high culture throughout the Islamic world. Even when it was eventually eclipsed, by English and then Urdu and Hindi in India, and by Turkish and Arabic in the post-Ottoman provinces, its impact was still felt on many levels: Urdu literature still follows Persian models, while trendy Westerners read the mystical writings of Rumi (d. 1273), about whom it was said, 'He has brought a [Holy] Book, though he is not a prophet'. Persian literature also found fans in Goethe (*West-Eastern Divan*) and Puccini (*Turandot*), amongst numerous other Western authors.

The Persians clearly have a lot of which to be proud, as imperial leaders in pre-Islamic times and as cultural and administrative leaders in Islamic ones. The late arrival of indirect Western domination to Iran in 1907 (when the country was divided into spheres of influence by Britain and Russia) ensured that Iranian patriotism has never really been weakened. Moreover, the resistance of the Persian people to the spread of Arabic, together with Iran's Shiite identity, have contributed to feelings of national uniqueness for centuries.

The flipside to all of this is that when Iran's position in the world has fallen short of national ambitions and expectations, rationalizations occasionally have been sought in strange (and dangerous) places. From the beginning of the 20th century, when foreign intervention in the country was at its height, conspiracy theories linking Iran's woes to secret plots by the Russians, British, Americans, Crusaders/Christians, Zionists/Jews, Freemasons, Bahais, and Satan have circulated widely, even amongst the country's political and religious elites.

Some of these theories are less outlandish than others: the CIA *did* orchestrate the 1953 coup that overthrew the Iranian

7. Mural on the former American Embassy in Tehran, Iran. The mural suggests that there is an American–Israeli–Satanic conspiracy to control the world

government, but it is preposterous to suggest that Ayatollah Khomeini was a British or American agent, or that Jews and Freemasons have conspired since the beginning of time to spread Hellenism (!) at Iran's expense. What is beyond doubt is that Iran and the Persians have had a truly formative influence on the contours and contents of Islamic civilization. In many ways, though, they could not have done it without the Turks.

The Turks

The Turks' involvement with Islamic history is full of surprises, almost all of which are pleasant. The first surprise is that they ever came to be involved at all. In their pre-Islamic history, Turks had created a series of empires (c. 552–840, and in western regions of the Eurasian Steppe into the 10th century) and adopted a number of religions along the way, including Manichaeism, Buddhism, Nestorian Christianity, and Judaism, as well as retaining the traditional forms of shamanism. Moreover, unlike the Arabs and Persians, the Turks were not native to the Near East, their original homeland being in Mongolia. As nomads of the Eurasian Steppe, they lingered on the edge of settled civilizations, plying the routes from east to west and occasionally creating states of their own. The empire of the Uyghur Turks (744–840), for instance, had close relations with the Chinese, exchanging horses for silk (at rates favourable to the Turks), and entering into occasional marriage alliances with the Chinese ruling families. As the Huns in earlier centuries and the Mongols in later ones, their ultimate target was Chinese civilization; had they been given a choice in the matter, the Turks probably would have joined the sedentary world in China rather than the Near East. Thus, when they first entered the Islamic world it was against their will, as military slaves in the 820s.

It is important to note that despite being bound by ethnic and linguistic ties, 'the Turks' consist of numerous loosely related groups: even today related, but essentially independent, Turkic peoples are widely dispersed across Asia, from Turkey through southern Russia, Iran, Central Asia, to western China or 'East Turkistan'. And while Turks *first* entered the Islamic world as young slave-soldiers, later Turks entered freely, after being converted in the late 9th century by merchants and Sufi leaders (who must have resembled the shamans of their own religions). In the case of the Qarakhanids in Transoxania (r. 992–1212), the Islamic world came to the Turks. In most other cases, however, it was the Turks who came to the Islamic world.

The second surprise is that Turkish slave-soldiers (*ghulam*s), fiercely loyal to their caliph and lacking political ambition, quickly came to dominate the Abbasid court in the 9th century and eventually establish their own states, from the Mamluks in the west (who were Ayyubid *ghulam*s) to the Ghaznavids (Samanid *ghulam*s) and Delhi Sultans (Ghurid *ghulam*s) in the east. Of great political significance were those Turks who came to the Islamic world from a position of strength, as invaders who rose to power and prominence in the old-fashioned way – by combining diplomacy, strategy, a unifying ideology, and military might. The Saljuqs, Ottomans, Mughals, and Safavids all belong to this category. When the caliphs al-Ma'mun and al-Mu'tasim began importing Turks to Islamic lands in the 9th century, they never would have guessed that the last people to hold the caliphal office – when it was abolished by the Ottomans in 1924 – would be (free-born) Turks.

Thus, for over a millennium, most Muslims lived under the rule or protection of Turks. It is not surprising, then, that Turkish terminology and administrative practices have left their stamp on Islamic history, particularly in the classical and early modern periods. In fact, the word for 'stamp' in modern Arabic, *damgha*, is an ancient Turkish word (originally pronounced *'tamgha'*), having meant 'tribal brand' in pre-Islamic times and 'commercial tax' in the Mongol period. The fortuitous journey of this word, from ancient Mongolia to the modern Arab world, neatly illustrates the scope and range of the Turks' activity in history.

The third surprise (to History but not, by now, to us) is that the Turks often chose to spread and develop Persian rather than Turkish literature. They *did* produce their own literary works: the earliest Turkish documents date from the 8th century and by the 11th century, Islamo-Turkish works were being composed, two of which – a mirror for princes from 1068 and an Arabic-Turkish lexicon from 1077 – are widely known. Despite this, the Turks relied on Persians in all things literary, a fact that is captured in a proverb recorded in the 11th-century lexicon, according to which, 'There is no Turk without an Iranian, just as there is no hat without a head'. Beginning in the 14th century, and increasing in the following one, literature in both western (Ottoman) and eastern (Chaghatay) Turkish came to be composed at Turkish courts. Hence, Babur's memoirs were composed in Chaghatay, though the high culture at the Mughal court was Persian. Still, it is ironic that one of the founders of Turkish literary culture, 'Ali Shir Nava'i (d. 1501), wrote a polemical work on the superiority of Turkish over Persian, the vocabulary of which is nearly two-thirds Persian.

Two further surprises, both of which come from the realm of culture, are the fact that the 'crescent and star' symbol with which Islam is often associated is of ancient Turkish (rather than Arab or Persian) provenance, and also that Turks have literally nourished Islamic (and other) civilizations through their culinary influence. Yoghurt, stuffed vine-leaves (*dolma*), kebabs, shawarma, and baklava, amongst many other well-known foods, all originate with the Turks (though Turkish coffee does not). And if the story is true that the croissant was created by Viennese bakers in celebration of the failed Ottoman siege of their city in 1683, then – at least indirectly – we owe them croissants too.

A final surprise is that a people such as the Turks who have long been associated with military prowess have always been remarkably tolerant of, and open to, other cultures and religions. Perhaps because of their travels along the Eurasian Steppe Route,

Turks have been exposed to numerous unrelated cultures in a way that some other nomads were not. (By contrast, during their own seasonal migrations, the Arabs came into contact with peoples to their north, south, and east – to their west was the Red Sea – who were basically sedentary versions of themselves.) For this reason, the Turks have a long history of willingly incorporating elements of other cultures into their own, as demonstrated by their adoption of others' letters – not only in the figurative sense of the word, with Persian high culture, but also literally, going through various alphabets until they accepted the Arabic script, like other Muslim peoples. Significantly, their capacity to adapt to changing circumstances has led them, unlike the Arabs or Persians, to adopt a Latin alphabet in the 20th century, a change undertaken not only by Turks in Turkey, but also those in Uzbekistan, Turkmenistan, and Azerbaijan. In a sense, the Turks have shown themselves to be both experts at identifying winning trends and flexible enough to align their own societies with them. This may be seen in their adoption of Islam, of Persian as a literary language, of gunpowder (against the grain of their indigenous traditions), and of modernity. Arabs and Persians may protest that they are too proud of their traditions to abandon them under pressure from outsiders, but the Turks can retort that in adopting and adapting to the prevailing culture – in this case, modernity – they too are remaining true to their traditions.

Conclusions

Muslim jurists since the 9th century have referred to the Islamic world as being a 'house' or 'abode' of Islam (*dar al-islam*). Though the sources do not extend the metaphor, I am tempted to do so. Accordingly, the land on which the house was built was first 'acquired' by Arabs, who also provided the house's architectural plans and foundations. Most of the house's bricks and builders were Persian, and for much of Islamic history, from the 9th to the 19th centuries, its landlords were Turks (who also contributed to the menu and welcome-mat). Shiites, for their part, have long believed that the house was built on shaky foundations, and nowadays the building has been divided into individual apartments of varying sizes. Since the 18th century, the interior design has been dominated by Western styles which, in some flats, clashed with the traditional décor, creating spots of ugliness. Islamists might say that the apartments are little more than seedy motel rooms in need of urgent attention, for which they hope to raze the whole building and rebuild it as a house. What this extended metaphor attempts to demonstrate is how the various peoples of Islamic history have interacted and combined to build something in which they all have a significant stake and to which they all contributed, albeit in different ways.

Chapter 3
Institutions

From the story of Islamic history we learn how diverse Muslim societies have been over time. We also learn that the fortunes of Muslims and Islam have fluctuated according to period and region – sometimes within the same period and region. Even if we limit ourselves to a particular time and place, there are various yardsticks against which Muslim societies can be measured: for all the talk of 'golden ages' – under the Rashidun, early Abbasids, Andalusian Umayyads, or whenever – conversion to Islam, Muslim cultural productivity, and Islamic political rule rarely coincided anywhere.

To an extent, this striking diversity can be explained by identifying the different peoples who feature in the story, each carrying their own cultural baggage. Constraints of space, however, have forced us into some (hopefully forgivable) generalizations: of course not all Turks are open-minded just as not all Persians are fiercely proud of their venerable culture. Another way of explaining and illustrating this diversity is to examine institutions that have been common, in theory, to all Muslim societies, while being different, in practice, in the various regions and periods of Islamic history. The three case studies chosen here are the mosque, *jihad*, and the caliphate (or 'imamate'). The first is a physical institution, the second a religio-legal one, and the third is both physical and religio-legal.

The mosque

In the first episode of the celebrated British television series on art history, *Civilisation*, Lord Clark remarked that Greco-Roman buildings are characterized by:

> the same architectural language, the same imagery, the same theatres, the same temples; at any time for 500 years you could have found them all round the Mediterranean – in Greece, Italy, Asia Minor, North Africa, or in the south of France…This building…is a little Greek temple that might have been anywhere in the Greco-Roman world.

Some of the earliest mosques built in the conquered provinces also had Greco-Roman architectural features, but rather than indicating that Islamic culture was the heir to Classical traditions, such mosques show precisely the opposite. Muslim rulers did not attempt to impose a uniform (Greco-Roman) building style everywhere they went; it was the local traditions that influenced the Muslims, who adapted existing buildings – and, when starting from scratch, building materials and techniques – to their needs. Accordingly, Greco-Roman traditions influenced Muslim architecture only in lands conquered from the Byzantines.

What does a mosque need? Strictly speaking, there are two types of mosque, the *masjid*, or 'place of worship' (from which, via the Spanish *mezquita*, the word 'mosque' is derived), and the *jami'*, a town's congregational mosque which, as the word indicates, gathers Muslims together for prayers and other religious functions. As a place of worship, mosques first and foremost require worshippers and prayer-leaders. Although some worshippers remain in the mosque between prayers (even eating and sleeping there), these people are perhaps part of the mosque's furniture but not its architecture. The building itself requires an area where ritual ablutions can be undertaken before prayer

8. A West African mosque (Djenne, Mali)

9. Muslims at the Niujie mosque (Beijing, China)

10. The Hassan II mosque (Casablanca, Morocco)

(including the necessary pure-water fountain); a *mihrab* ('niche') that indicates the location of Mecca, towards which Muslims pray; as well as, usually but not always, a *minbar* ('pulpit') from which sermons are delivered and a minaret from which Muslims are called to prayer five times daily.

Unsurprisingly, the largest mosque in the world is the great mosque in Mecca, built around the Ka'ba, to which millions of pilgrims flock every year. Somewhat less predictably, the second largest is said to be the Hassan II mosque in Casablanca, Morocco. Completed over a seven-year period (1986–93), by more than 6,000 people (often working day and night), the mosque can accommodate 25,000 people indoors and has the world's tallest minaret (c. 700 feet). With its glass floor (partially built over water), automated sliding roof, laser-beams that point to Mecca during night-time prayers, heated marble floors, electric doors, carved and painted ceilings, and white granite columns and glass chandeliers imported from Italy, it is an astounding building by any measure. Equally astounding is the fact that its 800 million

dollar cost was shouldered *entirely* by the people of Morocco
(even the poor).

As far as Islamic law is concerned, mosques are basically
unnecessary. All a Muslim needs to perform the prayers is the
wherewithal for ablution, a clean surface on which to prostrate,
and an idea of Mecca's location. Thus, visitors to the Muslim
world are likely to see large groups of men praying in the streets
of cities on a Friday at noon. Why, then, build mosques at all? And
why spend $800,000,000 on them? To the first question jurists
have long provided a number of answers, stressing the extra
potency of communal prayers and the special significance of holy
sites (such as Mecca and Medina, just as Jews pray at the Wailing
Wall though, like Muslims, they believe that God is everywhere).
The answer to the second question is more complex. Clearly a
mosque is more than just a prayer-hall. There are two further
roles of great historical significance that mosques have played
over the centuries. The first is as a symbol of triumph and power,
aimed at Muslims and non-Muslims alike; the second is as a
practical tool for the communication of ideas within the *umma*.

Over the centuries, when Muslims conquered lands, they were
free to build mosques almost anywhere they liked. In fact, to the
extent that Islamic law safeguards non-Muslim churches and
temples (so long as they do not overshadow Muslim ones), the
only places off-limits to Muslims in this context should be the sites
of existing houses of worship. And yet, the Islamic world – from
the 7th to the 21st centuries – is full of mosques that had once
been churches and temples. The al-Aqsa mosque and the nearby
Dome of the Rock were built on the Temple Mount in Jerusalem,
the Umayyad mosque in Damascus previously had been the
church of St John (and prior to that a Roman temple), and the
Hagia Sophia of Constantinople was converted by Mehmed II
into the Ayasofya of Istanbul (to complete the story, in 1935 it was
converted again … into a museum). There are literally hundreds of
examples of this process, as well as numerous cases in which the

traffic flowed in the other direction: during the Crusades, mosques (many of which had originally been churches) were converted [back] into Christian places of worship, only to revert to mosques once the Franks were evicted from the Holy Land in 1291. Similarly, the Mezquita in Cordoba was built in the 10th century on the site of what had been a temple and then a church, until in the 1230s it was *Reconquista*-d into a church (and continues to function as one today).

Mosque-building was thus an effective method of sending the message of Islam's triumph over other religions. Removing a competing culture's most prominent presence in a town sends a clear signal that the balance of power has shifted away from the older tradition, and recalculates the scorecard in Islam's favour. Most people want to be on the winning side of history and the conquest of lands and landscapes was usually followed by the large-scale conversion of local peoples. A mosque's triumphalist message could also be aimed at Muslims themselves, and numerous examples survive of architecturally unique mosques whose construction was intended to make a specific impression on local Muslims. Thus, it is most likely that 9th-century Iraqi Muslims, who witnessed the construction of the Samarra mosque and its minaret, associated the building's form – consisting of typically Mesopotamian mud-bricks in the shape of an ancient Babylonian ziggurat – with ancient Near Eastern traditions of divinely sanctioned monarchs who could ascend to heaven to speak directly to the gods.

Since the earliest times, Muslim rulers have used mosques to transmit important political messages to distant Muslim communities. A caliph's local representative had the community's attention when people gathered at the *jami'* on Fridays and religious festivals, and in these circumstances he could broadcast official messages reliably. Similarly, it was through the weekly prayers that local communities pledged allegiance to their caliph by mentioning his name in the *khutba* ('sermon'). Failing to insert

11. The spiral minaret of the Great Mosque of Samarra (Iraq)

12. The ziggurat of Agar Quf (Dur Kuigalzu, Iraq). This ziggurat was built by the Kassites (r. 1531–1155 BCE) and was partially restored by the Iraqi government in the 1970s

a ruler's name or, worse yet, attempting to insert a rival's name, was the easiest way to rebel against the authorities. Nowadays, Muslim political leaders, who seek to reach the largest possible audience, have mostly abandoned this means of communication with their subjects, resorting instead to modern media. Rather than being discontinued, the role of mosques as a gateway to the faithful has been taken up by Islamists, whose usual audience is likely to consist of mosque-goers anyway, and who take full advantage of the mosque's inviolability. No politician, even the most uncompromising dictator, wants to be seen to crack down on mosques, and even anti-establishment messages can be transmitted within their walls with impunity.

Not only is the mosque a symbol of Islam's diversity, it also typifies how 'organic' Islamic culture is. Mosques in China look *Chinese* rather than Arabian, Syrian, Iraqi, or Greco-Roman. Mughal-era and Ottoman-era mosques are easily distinguishable, although both are, at least superficially, the products of the same

Turco-Islamic culture. In fact, Mughal mosques mix Islamic and Indian elements, while Ottoman mosques mix Islamic and Byzantine ones. Even when mosque-building was a way of asserting Islam's victory over other religions, Islam and its monuments were defined in direct relation to those of local religious traditions. Whereas the Romans were bullish in stamping out other cultures' architectural traditions, Muslims have always been conscious of local contexts and have integrated features of earlier societies into their own, often creating a unique blend between old and new styles. In a way, Islam is the first 'green' civilization (though, it should be admitted, inadvertently so), with a long history of recycling older materials and using, for the most part, only local products and traditions. This is *not* why hippies read Rumi, but it surely cannot hurt.

Jihad

Rumi-reading hippies are less enamoured with *jihad*, support for which can come from other unexpected places: the former Israeli Prime Minister Ehud Barak and the British Member of Parliament Jenny Tonge have stated that had they grown up enduring the conditions under which Palestinians live, they would have 'become a suicide bomber' (Tonge) or 'joined a terrorist organization' (Barak). Unless Barak and Tonge were closet Muslims in their hypothetical scenarios, they are likely to be wrong about this. Although the motivations of suicide bombers are undoubtedly complex, it is clear that joining their ranks requires the fulfilment of two criteria: 1) The perpetrator must be seething about something; and 2) the option of assuaging one's anger through violence must be available and dogmatically justifiable to her/him. In the Palestinian case, it is the general category of *jihad*, to which suicide bombings are thought to belong, that provides the requisite justification. This explains why although thousands of Christian Palestinians live under the same miserable conditions (and millions of non-Muslim Indians and Africans endure far worse), they do not resort to such tactics. Of course, the overwhelming majority of Muslims do not support, let alone resort to, suicide bombings (often strongly condemning them) and non-violent interpretations of *jihad* have circulated amongst Muslims for centuries. In fact, the institution of *jihad* is an excellent example of Islamic history's great diversity, with countless rulers, scholars, religious groups, and entire societies interpreting the *jihad*-duty in their own ways.

On the face of it, there should be little scope for these competing interpretations of *jihad*, both because the Quran talks about it (though in ambiguous terms) and because '*jihad*' is a typical Arabic word. Arabic words consist of a consonantal (usually tri-literal) root and a set of patterns or verbal forms into which the root is inserted. Both the roots and the patterns have basic meanings: in our case, the root *j.h.d.* has to do with 'striving'; the word *jihad* itself is a noun derived from the third verbal form, whose basic meaning is 'to do something to (or against) someone'. Thus, *jihad* literally means 'striving against another'. The Quran tells us that the striving is to be done 'in the path of God', and against 'polytheists' (9: 5) or 'People of the Book', unless they fulfil certain conditions (9: 29). Taken together, *jihad*'s basic meaning might be 'religious striving against polytheists and [certain groups of] other non-Muslims'. Let's just stick with '*jihad*'.

Though it may seem straightforward, this definition has lent itself to many (often conflicting) interpretations, for a number of reasons. First, Muslims rarely if ever derive religious instruction directly from the Quran. It is through the analyses of the '*ulama*', who made sense of Quranic verses and rationalized them with other sources of religious law, that *shari'a* was formulated. Most of these scholars say that *jihad* means 'warfare aimed at spreading Islam', a phrase that itself is open to interpretation. Was Islam's spread meant to achieve political power over others (as with the Romans and Mongols) or converts to the religion (as with Buddhists and Christian missionaries)? All agreed that the answer was 'both', with conversion being the priority and political power seen as a stepping stone towards eventual conversion. It was also agreed that undertaking a *jihad* is the duty of the community as a whole – though individual Muslims were free to pursue their own *jihad*s to secure divine favour, irrespective of communal efforts. What evaded consensus are questions about the targets of *jihad* and the circumstances in which it is to be waged (amongst other issues). Apostates from Islam are fair game by everyone's reckoning, but what about Jews and Christians, Hindus, pagans, and – crucially for many in the West – atheists and apostates from *other* religions? Most authorities take a generous view of things and accord 'tolerated non-Muslim' status to a wide range of groups. At the other end of the spectrum, some extremists view all non-Muslims, and even those Muslims who disagree with them on points of theology or law, as infidels who must be defeated. And some scholars hold that *jihad* is to be undertaken as a Muslim initiative, whereas others feel it should be undertaken only in reaction to external provocation.

Second, as anyone who watches cars go by on the street knows, the letter of the law is not always applied in practice; thus, even if all Muslim scholars were to agree on everything, realities on the ground would manifest diversity (and once precedents are created, they have a way of replicating themselves). Hence, geographically, it was easier for rulers in Anatolia, Iberia, and India, for instance, to expand Islam's borders than for rulers in Arabia or Iraq. Politically, the dictates of law-books written under a strong caliphate could not be adhered to when the state was weak, and the realities of *jihad*-waging frequently clashed with legal theory.

Third, the assorted approaches to religion that developed over the centuries have cleared the way for multiple interpretations of *jihad*. From the 9th and especially the 10th centuries, many Muslims – influenced by quietist trends (e.g. Twelver Shiites), by spiritual ones (Sufis), and by Christian attacks against Islam's claim to be a religion of peace – came to divide *jihad* into two types. The first was what they termed the 'lesser *jihad*',

which is the familiar obligation to spread Islam at the expense
of other religions, but which is only to be undertaken as a
defensive measure. The second is the 'greater *jihad*', a general
obligation on all Muslims actively to ward off their own evil
inclinations. Though this distinction was retroactively attributed
to Muhammad himself, it is clear from the historical record
that most rulers (and many Muslims) disagreed with such
interpretations. The important point, though, is that they were
there to be adopted by those who abhor even defensive violence,
and – latterly – by Muslim apologists who claim that *jihad* has
been defensive or an inner struggle all along.

Finally, even if one were to settle on a particular interpretation
of the *jihad* obligation – say a lenient one according to which a
physical *jihad* is only a defensive measure and one that should
never target innocent civilians – the terms involved might still
be read in completely different ways. The lenient interpretation
used here will certainly appeal to the overwhelming majority of
Muslims, for whom *jihad* is a personal battle against temptation,
and who will be drawn into physical warfare only when provoked
by those threatening Islam itself. And even then, innocents will
be spared. The point of interest is that extremists such as those
behind the '7/7' attacks on London's transport system in 2005
are also likely to sign up to this lenient-sounding interpretation.
But to extremists, Islam *is* under attack (evidenced by the short-
sighted use of the phrase '*war* on terror' used by some Western
governments), a defensive *jihad* therefore *is* necessary, and those
non-combatants who were killed in the attacks were not innocent
at all – in democracies, voters bear full responsibility for their
government's actions (in this case, Britain's aggression (as they see
it) against Muslims in Iraq and Afghanistan).

The extremists' main selling-point is thus the insistence that
global *jihad* efforts are defensive. This makes *jihad* immediately
attractive to Muslims who may feel beleaguered by something –
Western culture, the non-Muslim societies in which they live,

or the course of history (which they feel is passing them by, even though their ancestors once ruled the world). If Muslims in Western countries feel that they are being subjected to Islamophobia, or are otherwise prevented from practising Islam, then they are obligated to create the conditions necessary for the upholding of *shari'a*, ideally by creating an Islamic state where one does not yet exist. To some Islamists (such as Osama bin Laden and his supporters), an acceptable Islamic state does not exist anywhere and a caliphate must be created from scratch and by force. Thus, to understand al-Qaeda's *jihad* we must grasp the (somewhat slippery) nature of the caliphate itself.

The caliphate or 'imamate'

Many, if not most, Islamist groups wish to establish a caliphate – a pan-Islamic state led by a 'caliph'; for some (such as *Hizb ut-Tahrir*, 'The [Islamic] Liberation Party'), its establishment is their sole aim. It is likely that many mainstream Muslims would theoretically welcome a renewal of the caliphate, but feel that it is not for them to bring this about. Islamists believe that *jihad* must be waged by the community as a whole, to expand the borders of an Islamic state. But seeing as there *is* no Islamic state and no 'community as a whole', the aim of *jihad* must – for the present time – be to create them. Even for those Muslims who see *jihad* as meaning little more than refraining from pork pies or inappropriate computer games, the idea of living under a caliphate has much to recommend it. It is only under caliphal rule that Muslims will be truly free to practise their religious traditions unapologetically. Furthermore, the caliphate would unite the *umma*, thereby unlocking the Muslim world's awesome political, economic, and military potential. The ills of modern Muslim societies, Islamists tell us, are entirely due to divisions within the *umma* – the artificial borders imposed by Western powers, the variety of governments (all bad) under which Muslims live (again, part of a Western plot), and so forth. By uniting the *umma*, a caliphate would restore the Muslims to world leadership. What's not to like?

Nothing, of course, and the problem is not that Muslims throughout history have rejected the idea of the caliphate, but that they could not agree on its form and details. The irony is that rather than unifying the *umma*, disputes about the caliphate have done more to fragment it – politically and theologically – than any other idea or institution. To that extent, the caliphate is an ideal example of the diversity of Muslim societies and Islamic history.

Muhammad died in 632, having been the religious and political ruler of the Muslim state since it was created in 622, and clearly someone else had to take charge of affairs in his absence. But who would this be, and how would he be chosen? One solution proposed was that the communal elders should get together and choose the most suitable candidate from amongst Muhammad's tribe (Quraysh). This is what Sunnis think, and such a consultation (*shura*) is the basis on which some of the earliest caliphs were selected. But what if Muhammad himself, with God's inspiration, had actually nominated a suitable successor in his lifetime? Shiites believe that this is what happened and that 'Ali was chosen; according to them the office passes through 'Ali's direct descendants from one generation to the next. As seen in Chapter 1, Shiites could not always agree on the precise line of the imam's descent, which created further schisms. What if 'Ali turned out to be a disappointing leader, as those who would become the Kharijites thought? For them, the caliph should simply be the most suitable candidate for the job, regardless of lineage (and when 'Ali turned out not to be the one, they killed him). Others thought that a leader's ability to take control of the state should be the decisive factor. After all, if God is guiding events, and He brings power into the hands of a particular person or family, who can argue? This was the Umayyad point of view. The list can be greatly extended, but the point should be clear: not only did the caliphate fail to unite the *umma*, it was the chief cause of divisions within it. And instead of unleashing the *umma*'s collective power, Muslims throughout the course of Islamic history have expended much of their intellectual and physical energies fighting amongst themselves about it.

There is also great diversity of opinion in Islamic scholarship about the nature of the institution. What was the role of the caliph (or 'imam', this being the term employed in Sunni theory as well as in Shiite practice)? Political rule of the *umma* was a given, but what about religious leadership? Some, including the Umayyads, early Abbasids, and Shiites, also assumed that the caliph/imam had religious authority. This assumption is supported by the fact that the disagreement about the caliph's qualifications produced sects rather than political parties. Others, such as the *'ulama'* and the post-*mihna* Abbasids (with one or two exceptions in the 12th century), disagreed. And what was to be done when one knew who the caliph/imam is – as Shiites do or did – but political rule of the *umma* is in the wrong hands? Wait until God restores power to His imam, or set about effecting this immediately? This problem was solved for many Shiites when their chosen imam disappeared in the late 9th century, inducing quietism. Other Shiites, whose imams continued to exist, usually adopted activism, most famously under the Fatimids.

From the mid-10th century, the prestige of the caliphal office took a sharp knock. In Abbasid lands, with the Shiite Buyids in charge, the (Sunni) caliph was reduced to being a legitimizing figure for *de facto* rule by others. Around the same time, counter-caliphates emerged, under the Fatimids and Andalusian Umayyads. By the 13th century, the office was further devalued, with the Mongol eradication of the Abbasid caliphate in Iraq and the Mamluk installation of a 'shadow' Abbasid caliph in Cairo. Oddly, this caliph, in turn, sanctioned the caliphal status of others, most notably the Ottomans (who could not claim to have suitable pedigree, as they trace their lineage not to Quraysh but to a she-wolf, as the ancient Romans did). The Abbasid caliph in Cairo even appointed other caliphs whose office coincided with his own: in 1484, the Mamluk-Abbasid caliph conferred the title 'caliph' on 'Ali Ghaji ibn Dunama (r. 1476–1503), the ruler of Bornu, having done the same for the Songhay ruler Askiya Muhammad (r. 1493–1528) a few years earlier.

When a caliph's detractors wanted to diminish his claims to legitimacy, they usually called him a 'king'. In the Quran, kingship is reserved for God, while in Muhammad's lifetime those men who bore the title were autocratic infidels, such as the Byzantine Caesar and Sasanid Shah. Although from the 10th century ancient titles were revived in Persian lands, including that of 'king', it is only under Western influence that Muslim rulers to the west of Iran have voluntarily assumed this title for themselves, starting with Sharif Hussein ('King of the Hijaz' from 1916) and his son Faisal (king of Syria and then of Iraq). Soon there were Muslim kings in Egypt, the Hijaz, and the merged region of Najd-Hijaz, known since 1932 as the Kingdom of Saudi Arabia. Morocco, Libya and Jordan followed suit. To Islamists, this is further proof of the 'Westoxification' of Islamic lands; the existence of a 'kingdom' ruling over Mecca and Medina is particularly galling, and it is not surprising that organizations such as *Hizb ut-Tahrir* are banned in Saudi Arabia.

Throughout Islamic history men have claimed to be other sorts of divinely sanctioned leaders of the *umma*. Some of these have declared themselves to be messianic saviours (*mahdi*s; from a long list of options, the Mahdi of Sudan, in 1881–89, is perhaps the most famous) while others have been mere religious reformers, such as the Mughal sultan Akbar and the Afsharid ruler of Iran, Nadir Shah (r. 1736–47). Still others combined the attributes of various leaders: Wallace Fard Muhammad, the founder of the Nation of Islam, claimed to be both the awaited *mahdi* and the reincarnation of Jesus (with Elijah Muhammad as his prophet). Occasionally, the heterodox nature of a leader's claim was too much even for Islam's flexible structure to bear, resulting in the creation of separate religions, such as the Druze and Baha'i faiths.

If one of your goals in life is to meet a caliph/imam, do not despair – caliphs and imams are to be found even today: the Aga Khan IV is the current imam of the Nizari Ismaili community (the

49th in line from 'Ali); and the Ahmadiyya Muslim Community follows the caliph Mirza Masroor Ahmad (r. 2003–), fifth successor to Mirza Ghulam Ahmad who in 1889 claimed to be the *mahdi*, the second coming of Jesus, and a renovator (*mujaddid*) of Islam. Both the Nizari and Ahmadi movements are widespread, with millions of followers all over the world. Other, less widely accepted caliphs pop up from time to time, including Metin Kaplan (1952–), the self-styled 'Caliph of Cologne', who is serving a life sentence in a Turkish prison for attempting to overthrow the Turkish government and establish a caliphate (*Kalifatsstaat*) in its place.

It is worth considering that even successful attempts to restore rule over the *umma* to the rightful caliph/imam are almost always led, by the demands of actual rule, to abandon their initial claims and aims, and to regress into the same practices that they had decried in their revolutionary stage. Such was the case with the Abbasids, Fatimids, Almoravids, Safavids, and numerous others, in both Islamic history and world history more generally (regarding political revolutions). Current calls for the re-establishment of a caliphate follow predictable forms; it is the eventual shape of any future caliphate that is unpredictable.

Chapter 4
The sources

How do we know what we know about Islamic history? In theory, as 'Islamic' history is a branch of history more generally, the methods and tools used by historians of other societies are also available – to a greater or lesser extent – to historians of Islam. Naturally, the sources for each branch of history are particular to it, and our sources for some periods and regions are better than those for others: in some cases, we possess a small number of sources that tell us a lot; in other cases, an extraordinary glut of sources proves to punch well below its weight.

In 1977 and 1978, four books were published in which historians of Islam were told that they were doing their job poorly. Edward Said's *Orientalism* chastised Islamicists for – amongst other things – creating a field of study that is condescending towards and critical of the Muslim societies that they study. John Wansborough's *Quranic Studies* and *The Sectarian Milieu*, along with Patricia Crone's and Michael Cook's *Hagarism*, told Islamicists that they are not being critical enough (in the scholarly rather than judgemental sense of the word). Over the past three decades, scholars have been forced to engage with the ideas presented in these books, even if only to refute them. Broadly speaking, historians work with two types of written materials: primary sources (written by the people *under* History's microscope) and secondary sources (written by the people looking *through* the microscope). Said's work concerns secondary sources and will be discussed in the following chapter; Wansborough's and Crone/Cook's work concerns primary sources and will be discussed here.

Our sources for Islamic history after 1100 (following the chronology adopted in Chapter 1) are, for the most part, of the sort that will be familiar to historians of other societies. People in these centuries wrote many books about many topics and – once we read them – we can attempt to reconstruct and analyse the world they describe. Obviously, the careful historian will be on guard for misleading or biased accounts (or for what some might consider to be the inevitable biases that each author brings to his/ her writing), but otherwise the study of Islamic history will be broadly comparable to the study of European history, for instance. In fact, by this period, due to events described in Chapter 1, some of our sources for Muslim societies *are* European documents and accounts. Jean Chardin (d. 1713), for instance, left us the record of his travels from France to the Near East and Iran, a record that fills ten volumes. Similarly, Ottoman–European relations are known to us from European accounts as well as Ottoman ones. The same can be said for the Mediterranean societies of the immediately preceding periods, when Christians from southern Europe and Muslims from North Africa and the Near East interacted regularly, leaving plenty of literary and documentary traces of this interaction from which historians can now benefit. From this context comes of one of our most important resources for Islamic history, the Cairo Geniza. This source, the nature and contents of which have no parallels in European societies, is worth highlighting here.

The Cairo Geniza comprises some 250,000 fragments discovered in an Egyptian synagogue at the end of the 19th century. Jews (as well as Muslims) are reluctant to dispose of documents that contain references to God's name. For this reason, religious documents that are no longer considered useful (because they are torn or otherwise irrelevant) are deposited in a safe location. Jews in Fatimid Cairo appear to have extended these rules to documents that merely concern God or religious issues more generally, and even to documents composed in Hebrew (to them, Divine) characters. As the Jews of Muslim lands usually wrote in local languages (e.g. Arabic, Persian) using Hebrew characters, the Cairo Geniza came to comprise an exceptionally varied selection of documents pertaining to all aspects of life under Islam, in Fatimid Egypt, Palestine, and Syria, as well as in southern Europe, North Africa, Yemen, and other lands with which this Jewish community had contact. Whereas most sources from Muslim lands were written by the literate elite, Geniza sources are largely the record of daily life amongst ordinary people, and provide us with a richly detailed snapshot of Islamic history in the 11th to 13th centuries. Amitav Ghosh's *In an Antique Land* is a historical novel based on these documents; Shlomo Goitein's five-volume *A Mediterranean Society* is a masterly reconstruction and analysis of the world of those who contributed to the Geniza. The Geniza is thus our most important source for a bottom-up view of Islamic history.

The 800–1100 period from which many of the Geniza documents date is also when the top-down view is reflected in an enormous range of literary works, almost all of which are in Arabic (the occasional exceptions being Persian works from the east). Due in part to the paper revolution described in Chapter 1, and in part to the necessarily protracted course over which such complex and sophisticated traditions develop, practically every work of fundamental importance to classical Islamic law, theology, Quranic and *hadith* studies, and – crucially for us – historiography dates from this period; before then, only administrative documents were regularly written down. Significantly, even those works attributed to earlier authors were first committed to writing in this period. Muslims almost certainly *did* write things in the 600–800 period: parts of the Quran itself and some early Islamic poetry, for instance, can be dated on the basis of internal evidence (predominantly linguistic archaisms) to no later than the

8th century; but not much else. Ibn Ishaq (d. 767) transmitted to his students a biography (*sira*) of Muhammad, for instance, and people read it (in notebook form), talked about it, and reworked it. We know this not because Ibn Ishaq's *sira* survives but because one of these later re-workings of it – by Ibn Hisham (d. 833) – does. Even the pre-Islamic Arabian poetry that is known to us is pre-Islamic poetry *as remembered by 9th-century authors*. The literary sources from the 800–1100 period are thus of great significance to us for their recollection of things that happened in the preceding one. This raises all sorts of questions (occasioning, in turn, all sorts of answers) of immense significance for the study of Islamic history, as we will now see.

The sources for 600–800 (and their limitations)

In 1972, a Muslim 'Geniza' was discovered in Yemen, containing tens of thousands of Quranic fragments, some of which date to the late 7th and early 8th century. Until then, our earliest attestation of Quranic verses came from the Dome of the Rock in Jerusalem (c. 692), and early Islamic 'language' and culture more generally are known to us from thousands of extant documents (mostly papyri from Egypt) and coins from the 7th and 8th centuries. The papyri tell us something about the administration of Egypt from the first century of Muslim rule, indicating how the rise of Islam there did or did not change realities on the ground. Coins from all over the caliphate exist in substantial numbers, and tell us something about caliphs, governors, and minor rebels in distant provinces. The dates of a ruler's tenure, the titles he chose for himself, and the inscriptions he had imprinted on his coins all provide us with details relating to the political scene in a given time and place.

Even cumulatively, however, these sources cannot provide us with a continuous, detailed account of the first century or so of Islamic history. For this we must rely on the voluminous and consequently very detailed literary accounts of this period, written (at least

13. Gold 'tanka' of the Delhi Sultan Qutb al-Din Mubarak Shah I (r. 1317–21). Both the 'tanka' denomination of the coin and its square shape reflect pre-Islamic Indian influence. The Arabic inscription on the coin, in which the Sultan is described as 'the commander of the faithful' and 'the caliph', is unmistakably Islamic

in their present form) in the 800–1100 period. The Quran tells us surprisingly little about Muhammad and the rise of Islam; traditions about Muhammad and his Companions (known as *hadiths*) and biographies of Muhammad (*sira*) and accounts of the early Islamic conquests (*maghazi*) fill the gaps. Arabic chronicles are very detailed and contextualize the information of these other sources within their greater historical framework, often starting with the creation of the world and continuing into the 9th and 10th centuries. In terms of quantity, we are better served by sources that describe this period than are historians of Western Europe, Byzantium, India, or China, in the same period. That is the good news. The less-good news is that these sources are beset by historiographical issues, as identified (mostly but not exclusively) by modern scholars.

Even when Abbasid-era authors describe the first half of the 8th century (of which they may have had first-hand experience), their accounts must be filtered for anti-Umayyad propaganda. These sources are not only consciously pro-Abbasid but also (less consciously) pro-Eastern, that is to say they focus on Iran/

Iraq far more than they do on Syria, Egypt, North Africa, and Iberia (though these individual regions produced much smaller and less influential works of their own). Such biases are more or less understandable – why would Abbasid, Iraq-based historians of Persian descent (which, on the whole, is who they were) do otherwise? After all, everyone knows that history is written by the victors, and these victors were unencumbered by notions of political correctness. But Abbasid sources for early Islam are also problematic for less obvious reasons.

Imagine finding our Martian guest on your doorstep. The initial hurdle in trying to understand who he is, where he is from, and why he is there, is a linguistic one. Once we learn his language, we can then ask him all about himself. But what are we to make of his answers? Are we to assume that the standards of accuracy that we apply in the modern West are shared by Martians? Even if we decide that he is aware of our standards and sincere in his attempts to satisfy them, are we to expect him to remember anything about his birth and infancy or to have an unbiased (or otherwise untainted) opinion of his parents, family, and friends? And what are we to make of the numerous contradictions we may find in his testimony?

In some ways, dealing with the literary sources for the early history of world religions is even more difficult than dealing with the testimony of Martians. Our understanding of early Judaism and early Christianity (to take two examples) is compromised by deficiencies that obscure our picture of what happened in the formative period of these religions, chief amongst which are the fact that virtually no verifiably contemporary sources exist, and that these are histories whose theological, spiritual, and political stakes are exceedingly high (leading us to be sceptical about versions of events that might benefit those who recount them).

The study of early Islam is no different. Even if we assume that our later sources have transmitted their accounts accurately (an assumption to which we will return, with a magnifying glass, below), they still present us with two, related problems. First, they can be contradictory, in some cases offering us a dozen or so conflicting versions of a single event. Second, they usually relate to politically and religiously loaded issues, such as the right of a certain group to stipends from the state (precedence in converting to Islam, or involvement in the early conquests had direct financial ramifications for many Muslims), or the correct practice of Muslim rituals (if an historical account shows Muhammad or his Companions to have done things in a certain way, then those practices can serve as legally binding precedents). Thus, what might appear to us as 'secular' history is in fact largely shaped by religio-legal concerns. For this reason a great historian such as al-Tabari (whom we will encounter below) provided *several* versions of the same event, usually without expressing his own opinion on them: to be useful and impartial as an historian, he had to limit his task to the presentation of the existing options to his readers, who could marshal one of the versions in support of their point of view. Modern scholars have demonstrated that many of the conflicting *hadith*s or historical reports (*akhbar*) were created as part of a legal debate between local schools and their members, which would explain why al-Tabari had so many versions of events to record in his massive work.

Furthermore, we should not take it for granted that once language barriers are surmounted a text's meaning will be unambiguous to us. Ninth-century Arabic may be far more similar to 19th-century Arabic than modern English is to Old English, but literal understanding of an account's language does not guarantee an understanding of historical facts. Scholars have shown that Arabic accounts of this period (Muhammad's life and the early conquests in particular) are replete with *topoi* (sing. *topos*). A *topos* is a literary convention or device that is meant to make a point without being taken literally. For example, when a child boasts that her daddy is 'ten times stronger than Penelope's daddy', we know that in 99% of cases (itself a *topos*) the child did not measure the relative strength of hers and Penelope's fathers and reach a 10:1 ratio. 'Ten times stronger' is simply another way of saying 'a lot'. An example from early Islamic sources is the assertion that Muhammad received his first revelations at the age of 40. All but the most hypothetical of revisionists would agree that Muhammad lived past the age of 40, so he must have done *some* things in that year. To that extent, there is little reason to doubt this detail in the *Sira*. However, scholars familiar with Near Eastern cultures and languages from the centuries preceding and following the rise of Islam recognize that the age of '40' is a *topos* for 'spiritual maturity'. Saying that Muhammad began to receive revelations at this age is saying that he was spiritually mature, not that he was literally 40 years old. Accepting that '40' is a *topos* is innocuous as it has no bearing on Islamic beliefs and rituals. Modern scholars have identified dozens of such *topoi* in accounts of Muhammad's life and, especially, the early Conquests, and even if these too are hardly destructive to our understanding of Islamic history itself, they chip away at our confidence in the utility of these sources. In other words, what these sources are *saying* and what they are *telling us* is not always the same thing, and to understand them fully, we must study our sources within the context of Near Eastern languages and literatures from late antiquity, a process that is still in its infancy.

It has also been shown that early Arabic sources on the first century of Islamic history must be understood within the broader context of their genre. To assess the value of a particular account or work, it pays to be aware of earlier and later accounts of the same topic. Research along these lines has shown that early Arabic sources that are based on orally transmitted narratives dealing with the rise of Islam *increase* in volume and detail rather than *decrease* with time (contrary to what we might have expected, human memories and Chinese-whispers being what they are). This applies to details about Muhammad's life in both the *Sira* and in the *hadith* literature. Thus, Ibn 'Abbas is said in a late 8th-century work to have transmitted no more than ten *hadith*s; by the 9th century, he is said to have transmitted 1,710. Some of these may be the early handful of *hadith*s that he is thought to have transmitted, but which ones?

To answer this question, scholars have devised methods for sifting what they deem to be authentic historical reports and *hadith*s from fabricated ones. Before getting to these, it should be stressed that the debate about the authenticity of our sources for early Islamic history is often misrepresented as being between believers who trust the sources and unbelievers who do not. This is wrong for all sorts of reasons: we will see here and in the following chapter that there are and have been non-Muslims who take the early sources at face value, just as there are Muslims who apply the methods of critical scholarship to these sources. In fact, the 'critical' approach to the sources was pioneered by Muslims in the 9th century. The identification of foreign words in the Quran, a pursuit rejected by modern Muslims as a hostile 'Orientalist' enterprise, was first undertaken by Muslim lexicographers in the Abbasid period. More crucially, the process of identifying the small number of authentic *hadith*s from the huge mass of fabricated ones was pioneered and developed by Muslims. Thus, al-Bukhari (d. 870), the compiler of one of the six authoritative (to Sunnis) collections of *hadith*s, is said to have chosen his c. 7,400 'sound' *hadith*s from an original corpus of 600,000. About two-thirds of these 7,400 are repetitious, so the actual number of acts and statements attributed to Muhammad is considerably fewer than 3,000. Modern, sceptical scholars make much of the statistics here. Although these scholars overlook the fact that '600,000' is actually a Near Eastern *topos* for 'an enormous group in its entirety' (cf. *Exodus* 12: 37), the 7,400 *hadith*s must be still a mere fraction of the original corpus. How did al-Bukhari (and his colleagues) accomplish this?

Isnads – the traditional solution

To sift authentic accounts from spurious ones, Muslims in
the 8th and 9th centuries developed and applied a science of
isnad-analysis. Every *hadith* (and this applies to early historical
sources too) contains two parts: a *matn*, which is a statement
about something Muhammad or another early authority said or
did; and an *isnad* or 'chain of authorities' that serves as a sort of
Near Eastern footnote, telling us how each report has reached us
(e.g.: al-Tabari heard it from 'x', who heard it from 'y', who heard it
from 'z', who was an eyewitness to the event). *Isnad*-analysis was
taken so seriously that an entire auxiliary genre of biographical
literature was produced to determine whether the various links
in an *isnad* are reliable and likely to have transmitted from and
to other links in the chain. These biographical dictionaries can
be enormous and the genre is virtually unparalleled in other
historiographical traditions. Thus, for most Muslims the problems
concerning the sources for early Islam are basically solved in
the following way: a method (*isnad*-analysis) was devised; tools
(biographical dictionaries) were developed to enable scholars to
apply the method; reliable scholars (led by al-Bukhari and five
others in the case of *hadith*s, and al-Tabari and others in the case
of historical chronicles) did all the sifting work; and now we know
exactly what Muhammad did and said, and how the rest of early
Islamic history unfolded.

Much of this activity is owed, at least indirectly, to a scholar
by the name of al-Shafi'i (d. 820). Before him, Islamic law was
locally based, with each region having its own traditions and
authoritative jurists. The earliest *hadith*s were thus traced to the
leading lawyers of each regional tradition. Al-Shafi'i realized that
this variety was dangerous to the *umma*'s cohesion and introduced
two rules that were generally accepted by all schools of thought:
only *hadith*s traced back to Muhammad himself are to be followed
(thereby overriding idiosyncratic, local rulings); and such *hadith*s
must be followed (even, interestingly, when they contradict the

The sources

Quran, as Muhammad's sayings are taken to be divinely inspired 'living commentary' on the Quran itself). Following al-Shafi'i, various local schools started assembling *hadiths* with sound *isnads*, resulting eventually in the six collections taken by Sunnis to be authoritative. (The relationship between Shiite *hadiths* and Shiite law is much simpler, as *hadiths* attributed to the imams were transmitted from the very start, with relatively little regional variety.)

Modern scholars have identified problems with this process and its results and look to the *matn* of a *hadith* (as well as to the *isnad*) for evidence for or against a report's authenticity. Already in the late 19th century, Ignaz Goldziher (d. 1921) argued that *hadiths* tell us more about 8th- and early 9th-century legal debates than they do about Muhammad's life. His ideas were pursued by Joseph Schacht (d. 1969), who made two major points of his own. First, by examining a wide selection of early *hadiths*, he determined that only in the mid-8th century were *isnads* going back to Muhammad widely circulated. Second, he reasoned that the better an *isnad* conforms to al-Shafi'i's rules, the more likely it is to post-date those rules. Thus, not only do *isnads* traced back to Muhammad not prove a *hadith*'s authenticity, they almost certainly prove the opposite (at least regarding the *isnad* itself; it in turn may have been attached to a genuine statement).

Two further objections to the science of *isnad*-analysis have been raised: first, an *isnad* authenticated by traditional means can be cut-and-pasted onto any *hadith* or historical report for which one seeks a formal seal of approval. Second, the fact that some 'sound' *hadiths* were not adduced in 8th- and 9th-century debates to which they would have provided a definitive solution suggests that these *hadiths* simply did not yet exist. By contrast, modern scholars grant that a *hadith* concerning an issue that was obsolete by the late 8th century or one that goes against what became acceptable practice by all Muslims is likely to be genuinely ancient – even if these *hadiths* have deficient *isnads* (hence, in such cases modern scholars are *more* accepting of a report's authenticity than traditional Muslim scholars are).

What these scholars have in common with traditional Muslims is the conviction that *hadith*s and early accounts of the rise of Islam *do* contain useful data on the basis of which Islamic history can be reconstructed. Where they differ is in their means for identifying authentic reports. And, not having religious or theological concerns riding on the issue of authenticity (regardless of any cultural or political biases they may hold), modern scholars can allow themselves to presume *hadith*s to be inauthentic unless proven otherwise, whereas traditional scholars presume the opposite. Still, proponents of both approaches agree that *hadith*s and early historical reports *can* be proven to be 'innocent' and of use to historians.

Much of the above concerns the utility (or futility) of *isnad*-analysis. Since *isnad*s were used by both *hadith*-collectors and most early historians, in theory the issues are of relevance to all written accounts of the first two centuries of Islamic history. In practice, however, most modern scholarship on these matters has dealt specifically with *hadith*s, while being altogether more accepting of 'historical' accounts (i.e., those preserved in chronicles). It was only a matter of time before scholars would attempt to apply the same standards of scepticism to historical accounts as were applied to *hadith*s, which brings us to Wansborough's books and Crone/Cook's *Hagarism*. The basic idea of these studies is that although *Sira* accounts and chronicles of early Islamic centuries take a form that resembles 'real' historical sources – by following chronological sequences, being more or less internally consistent, and being full of names, dates, places, and verisimilar events (accounts of Muhammad's life are much freer of ostensibly fictitious elements than we might have expected) – they are open to the same objections raised against *hadith*s, and are too closely bound up in questions directly relating to Muslim beliefs and practices to be deemed as anything other than religious literature. Early Islamic history is thus not to be reconstructed on the basis of such sources.

Where Wansborough and *Hagarism*'s authors differ is in their responses to this problem. Wansborough argued that we simply cannot know how Islam arose and developed in the 7th and 8th centuries. Each of his works makes this point by focusing on a different set of sources: *Quranic Studies* deals with the Quran and early exegetical works, and *The Sectarian Milieu* is concerned with the early Islamic historical tradition. The latter identifies numerous *topoi* in Prophetic biographies, as discussed above, and argues that Islam emerged when the conquering Arabs sought to distinguish themselves from the Christians and Jews of the conquered populations. The former work asks a number of questions about the Quran itself: why does it contain contradictory verses and parallel passages? Why, following earlier arguments about *hadith*s, are Quranic verses not adduced as evidence in early legal debates to which they are clearly relevant? And why did exegesis of the Quran emerge only a century or so after the Quran is supposed to have been assembled into its classical form? (Most modern scholars reject the attribution to early 8th-century Muslims of exegetical works bearing their names.) To these and other questions Wansborough saw only one convincing answer: a definitive codex of the Quran does not predate the turn of the 9th century. More generally, he argued that just as Islamic literary culture, administration, and art emerged gradually, over centuries of contact between the Arab conquerors and the conquered populations of the Near East, Islam as a religion must also have developed gradually.

The authors of *Hagarism* also concluded that Islam and the Quran as we know them are not as 7th- and 8th-century Muslims knew them. They postulated, on the basis of non-Muslim sources from the period, that Mecca was not the original sanctuary of Islam; that the early conquests took place before Islam had emerged as a religion distinct from a form of Judaism; and that, accordingly, 'Islam' and 'Muslims' were not the original labels of the religion and its followers. Rather, Muslims were known by a word derived from the Semitic root *h.g.r.* (or *h.j.r.*), which referred both to the *HiJRa*, which was an Exodus from Arabia to the Holy Land (rather than a flight from Mecca to Medina), and to the Arabs' descent from Hagar, Ishmael's mother. Neither Wansborough's works nor *Hagarism* has met with widespread acceptance, both because their arguments are contentious (and, in light of recent evidence such as the Yemeni Qurans, on some points summarily refutable), and because modern approaches to Islamic history have been shaped by a fairly unique set of concerns and considerations that might discourage the pursuit of certain arguments about early Islamic history, as we will now see.

Chapter 5
Competing approaches

Although many Western historians of Islam are not Muslims, it would be difficult to determine this from their writings on the first centuries of Islamic history. This is in stark contrast to historians of Judaism and Christianity, who tend to adopt an outsider's approach to their subject when writing in academic contexts (despite often being themselves Jews and Christians). Why the difference? Before turning to answers, it is worth underlining the question. The traditional accounts of Islam's rise tell us that in a remote and isolated region of Arabia (the Hijaz), in a pagan town unaccustomed to monotheism (Mecca), an illiterate man (Muhammad) began to recite verses full of references to Biblical characters and established monotheistic ideas. If we accept this basic outline – and most do – how are we to explain Muhammad's acquaintance with these ideas? To traditionally minded Muslims, the answer is clear: God, via an angel, revealed the verses to him. In fact, it would be hard to be a believing Muslim in the traditional sense without accepting this version of events. Equally, however, Wansborough might argue that it would be hard to accept the broad outlines of the story without being a Muslim (or at least without accepting God's hand in these events), for which reason he argued that Islam and the Quran developed later and elsewhere, where Jewish and Christian ideas were prevalent. *Hagarism* attempted to recreate the circumstances of this subsequent religious development. As noted above, almost everyone agrees that both Wansborough and *Hagarism* are wrong on points of detail (though criticism of *Hagarism* focuses almost exclusively on the first part of the book; few reviewers seem aware that the second and third parts contain salient points about the development of Islamic civilization in its Near Eastern context that might repay further investigation). Although neither Wansborough nor *Hagarism* have offered entirely persuasive answers to the questions about the rise of Islam, why have the questions themselves been largely ignored?

For many scholars, these books are to be judged on the basis of their conclusions, and if the conclusions are wrong then everything associated with these works is also wrong. To sceptics, it is the methodology that matters: the answers proposed may be wrong but the questions still need to be answered (all the more so if previous answers have been deemed unsatisfactory). There is evidence to suggest that there are considerations at play that go beyond usual academic argumentation and debate. We should not be surprised, perhaps, that 'Hagarism' never caught on as a term for 'Islam', but why was 'Mohammedanism' abandoned in the second half of the 20th century? Until then, it was a perfectly acceptable word, consistent with 'Zoroastrianism', 'Buddhism', 'Confucianism', and the Persian term *musavi* ('Moses-ian') with reference to Jews. While this may sound pernickety and of little significance, the issue cuts through to larger questions of Islamic exceptionalism. Whereas historians of other religions start with historical models and read primary sources in their light, many historians of Islam start with Muslim sources and proceed to tidy them up – removing patently incredible materials (references to miracles, round numbers, and the like) and taking the remaining material at face value. Why are Islam, and Islamic history particularly, exempt from established rules of historical enquiry?

One answer is that both Islam and the study of Islamic history are relatively young. Islam's youth compared to Judaism and Christianity famously led Ernst Renan (d. 1892) to state that

Muhammad 'was born in the full light of history', a statement with which most scholars (including pre-modern Muslim ones) would take issue, and which is contradicted by the evidence of the previous chapter. Islamic history's youth is a plausible explanation for the tendency to credit traditional accounts unquestioningly: thus, a critical edition of al-Tabari's massive (and, for early Islamic history, indispensable) *History* was first published in the late 19th century; and a full translation of the work was completed in the late twentieth. Much of the work on Islamic history conducted in the late 19th and 20th centuries involved finding, editing, and deciphering primary sources, and producing basic analyses of their contents. Those few scholars, such as Julius Wellhausen (d. 1918), who were able at this early stage to analyse Islamic history critically, came to Islamic Studies from Biblical or Near Eastern Studies more generally, and their work on early Islamic history still tended to be far more conservative than their work on other religious cultures of the Near East.

Another answer is that accounts of early Islam such as those preserved in al-Tabari's *History* are very difficult to ignore, replete as they are with impressively detailed descriptions of the people and events that interest scholars and students. Disregarding ready-made answers to pivotal questions is particularly challenging in the absence of viable alternatives to traditional narratives. Understandably, most scholars would prefer to have an imperfect version of history than none at all. And once the traditional narrative is adopted in classrooms, a scholastic status quo sets in: the students who learn this traditional version of Islamic history become teachers themselves and perpetuate the narrative and methodology.

A third answer is that societal and political pressures have discouraged both Muslim and – for different reasons – Western historians from questioning traditional accounts of, and sources for, the rise and early development of Islam. Muslim historians who raise doubts about their tradition are sometimes seen by their coreligionists as more reprehensible than are Westerners who do so. After all, ever since early Muslims accused Jews and Christians of intentionally distorting God's scripture, such anti-Islamic shenanigans have been expected of non-Muslim scholars. But *Muslim* scholars, it is thought, really should know better. Hence, when Suliman Bashear (d. 1991) argued that Islam developed gradually, just as other religions did, his students at the University of Nablus (Palestine) threw him out of a second-storey window. And for suggesting that the Quran is a literary text and must be read as one, the Egyptian scholar Nasr Hamid Abu Zayd was declared an apostate and his marriage was accordingly annulled (he and his wife fled Egypt). Some seventy years earlier, in 1926, Taha Hussein (d. 1973) – a leading Egyptian intellectual and education minister – argued that much of pre-Islamic Arabian poetry is inauthentic, for which he too was branded an apostate (even though the idea is of only tangential relevance to the Islamic tradition). Such instances of scholastic intolerance are, of course, extremely rare, but the mere existence of a few well-publicized cases of the sort can have an intimidating effect on those within the Muslim world who might otherwise be inclined to adopt an outsider's approach to the study of Tradition.

Western scholars who study Islamic history, especially since World War II, have also been conscious of Muslim sensibilities. This is partly to do with recent academic trends, originating in the social sciences, which stress the importance of understanding 'the experience of the believer' above all else. And it is partly to do with attempts by recent scholars to redress the wrongs committed by past generations of Orientalists, which brings us to Edward Said's *Orientalism*.

Edward Said and *Orientalism*

In the early 1940s, Sati' al-Husri (d. 1967), a Syrian intellectual and leading proponent of Arab Nationalism, argued that Western books on 'Arab' history are 'biased and [used] as tools of the imperialists who have always attempted by all means available to suppress or distort historical consciousness in order to perpetuate their rule'. A related argument was put forward in *Orientalism*, a hugely influential work that helped establish post-colonial studies. Although the book is primarily about the Orient as reflected in literary works, it also zeroes-in on the careers of specific Orientalists (from c. 1800 onwards), and its three main points are about the field of Orientalism itself. The first point is that Orientalism has tended to be 'essentialist', assuming as it does that Arabs (and Muslims more generally, though Said is mainly concerned with Near Easterners) have an essential, unchanging nature that can be identified, described, and controlled politically. The second point is that Orientalism, especially as practised by British and French scholars, has been politically motivated. If the 'nature' of Arab or Muslim societies can be shown to be inferior to those of the West, then Western political domination of Arabs and Muslims can be justified. The final point is that these flawed impressions about the inferior essence of 'Orientals', and the need to consider the East only as it relates to the West, have been enshrined in a self-perpetuating and flawed field of study.

Although much of what Said argued was old news in both Western and Arab/Muslim intellectual circles, his work brought these issues to the attention of a much broader readership, comprised mostly of intellectuals from other fields. The publication of the book in 1978 also contributed to its popularity: this was a dynamic period in the fields of literary theory that focused on culture's role in dominating or subjugating politically weak elements of society (post-colonial and feminist theory being particularly prominent in this context). *Orientalism* was critically acclaimed in the field of Cultural Studies; amongst Orientalists themselves, however, it was predictably controversial.

Orientalism's critics, many of whom are leading scholars of Islamic history, have highlighted a number of flaws in the work, which challenge both its details and central theses. It was pointed out, for example, that in the 19th century, at the height of European colonial domination of the Muslim world, the field of Orientalism was dominated not by British or French scholars, but by German-speakers from countries that had no direct rule over Muslims anywhere. It was also noted that many British and French Orientalists at the time were unsupportive of their countries' policies. Thus, E. G. Browne (d. 1926), professor of Persian at the University of Cambridge, was openly critical of British attitudes and policies towards Muslims; for his efforts and achievements, a street in Tehran was named in his honour (where a statue of his likeness can still be seen). Another objection to *Orientalism* is that it ignores the many vital contributions that Orientalists have made to the field of Islamic Studies: producing critical editions of manuscripts, to name but one example, is a task that serves Muslims too and is not readily susceptible to political biases. Still, Western scholars working on Muslim societies could hardly ignore *Orientalism*, and even the book's detractors accept that its influence on the field of Islamic Studies has been significant: in recent decades, Islamic Studies has been guided by a conscious effort to empathize with Muslim societies – past and present – as well as a reticence to present historical arguments that might offend Muslims. The questions and ideas raised in Wansborough's works and *Hagarism* could not be expected to take root in such barren scholastic ground.

That Westerners studying Muslim societies should be compassionate and sensitive towards those peoples whom they study is surely laudable (and obvious). And yet, an unexpected consequence of *Orientalism*'s influence is that conscious attempts to 'be nice' can stifle open and serious academic debate, thereby preventing Islamic Studies from attaining the professional standing that other branches of Near Eastern Studies enjoy. This amounts to a condescending approach to a religio-historical tradition that deserves to be treated with the same respect that is afforded to comparable traditions. A scholar of Biblical history cannot give an academic paper on the historicity of baby Moses in a basket on the Nile River and expect to be taken seriously by colleagues in the audience. In most cases, however, a scholar of Islamic history can talk about the most traditional details of Muhammad's biography and receive warm smiles and polite applause. Treating Islamic Studies with an exceptionally soft touch, implies (even if not consciously) that Islam should not be subjected to the same rigorous analysis that other traditions have undergone, lest it does not prove sufficiently robust to withstand the scrutiny. Ironically, while this approach to the Muslim tradition is 'nice', its patronizing assumptions are closely related to the sort of Orientalism that Said criticized, though such an uncritical approach is normally adopted by fans of Said's arguments.

Marshall Hodgson and *The Venture of Islam*

There *are* ways of being 'nice' while maintaining professional academic standards. Perhaps the most striking example of this is the work of Marshall Hodgson (d. 1968). The two books for which Hodgson is known are *The Venture of Islam: Conscience and History in a World Civilization* and *Rethinking World History: Essays on Europe, Islam, and World History*, both of which were published posthumously, on the basis of research conducted in the 1940s, 1950s, and 1960s. *The Venture of Islam* is a three-volume comprehensive account of all periods and regions of Islamic history, considered within the wider context of world history. As such, the work is a forceful argument against Islamic exceptionalism – the rise and development of Islam and Islamic civilization are woven into a tapestry of global dimensions and are seen to conform to the trends of history rather than bucking them. This bird's-eye view of history led Hodgson to a number of original conclusions about both Islamic history and civilization, and about the methodology by which historians should study them. Although his work is a magisterial summary of the entire Orientalist tradition, in many ways it is also an attempt to identify and rectify the tradition's weaknesses. Whereas *Orientalism* was a critique of the tradition from the outside, *The Venture of Islam* is a critique from within.

There are many ways in which Hodgson anticipated Said's criticisms (and it is curious that *Orientalism* makes no reference to Hodgson's work). For instance, Hodgson repeatedly rejected essentialist approaches to Islam, stating that 'every generation makes its own decisions'. Moreover, he was so disturbed by Eurocentric approaches to Islamic history that he set about purging the field of notions and terminology borrowed from European history. For this purpose, he coined a series of neologisms to replace what he thought were culturally loaded, or otherwise imperfect, phrases that tainted the study of Muslim societies. The 'Middle East', a term that puts Europe at the centre of the world, thus became the 'Nile-to-Oxus region' and the Industrial Revolution became 'The Great Western Transmutation'. Yes, his solutions could be clunky and his categorizations abstruse ('idographic' and 'nomothetic'; 'typicalizer' and 'exceptionalizer'; 'admonitionist' and 'revisionist'; 'agrarianate' and 'technicalistic'; amongst others), but – as the work's subtitle implies – conscience and accuracy (rather than elegance) were the guiding forces in Hodgson's approach to Islamic history. And although computer spell-checks reject all of his neologisms, scholars have been more tolerant of some of them, such as 'Islamicate' with reference not to Islam as a religion but to 'the social and cultural complex historically associated with Islam and the Muslims'.

For his sensitive approach to the study of Muslim societies, and his effort to situate Islamic history within the big picture of world history, Albert Hourani (d. 1993) concluded that, 'Marshall Hodgson has given us a framework of understanding which may be no less valuable than that of his great ancestor Ibn Khaldun.'

14. Marshall Hodgson

15. Ibn Khaldun

al-Tabari and Ibn Khaldun

How did Muslim historians themselves view Islamic history? A short comparison of the lives and works of al-Tabari (838–923) and Ibn Khaldun (1332–1406) – arguably, the two greatest Muslim historians – presents us with two very different answers to this question. In many ways, the two approached Islamic history from opposite ends: al-Tabari was an easterner – an Iranian from Amul, south of the Caspian Sea; whereas Ibn Khaldun was a westerner – an Andalusian Arab born in what is now Tunisia. The former lived and worked during the high-point of Arabo-Islamic civilization; the latter during one of its low-points (his family fled the *Reconquista* to North Africa). And whereas al-Tabari was consciously detached from governmental circles and independent of political influence, Ibn Khaldun spent much of his adult life immersed in self-serving schemes and political machinations, which brought him into contact with such figures as the Castilian King Pedro ('the Cruel') and Timur.

It should not be surprising, then, that the different circumstances that shaped their respective historical works had an impact on their approaches to history. Expectedly, al-Tabari's work has much fuller accounts of eastern provinces than of western ones, and the reverse is true for Ibn Khaldun's writings. Moreover, as a Persian, al-Tabari exerted considerable efforts towards the reconciliation of ancient Persian and Judeo-Christian accounts of pre-Islamic history; Ibn Khaldun, for his part, was unconcerned about these things.

Less expectedly, perhaps, their perspectives on history's course, as well as its causes and effects, were radically different. Had he carried business cards, al-Tabari's would probably have said *faqih* ('jurist'), *'alim*, or something of the sort, rather than 'historian'. Indeed, in his day al-Tabari was best known as a leading religious scholar, is even said to have created his own school of Islamic thought (the 'Jariri *madhhab*'), and he is just as famous amongst

Muslims for his voluminous exegesis (*tafsir*) on the Quran as he is for his *History*. His view of Islamic history was thus heavily conditioned by religious concerns. To him, God created the world and, after c. 7,000 years (he explains the calculation in the introduction to his work), He will bring it to an end. History is in God's hands and its course is progressing inexorably towards the End of Times (an idea with both Iranian and Semitic pedigrees).

Ibn Khaldun, by contrast, saw history as the product of certain identifiable, dynamic processes, such as the interaction between barbarians imbued with 'tribal' cohesion (*'asabiyya*) and the settled civilizations that they bordered. Ibn Khaldun's theory of history dictates that the barbarians will occasionally unite to overrun neighbouring civilizations and become civilized themselves, only to be conquered by a new batch of barbarians as the process is repeated indefinitely. Thus, unlike al-Tabari's linear, teleological, God-driven narrative, Ibn Khaldun saw history as cyclical and subject to rules and patterns. This is the approach that modern historians and sociologists adopt and, to the extent that Ibn Khaldun created it, he may be regarded as the founder of these academic disciplines (though there is no evidence that their eventual founders were indebted to Ibn Khaldun). Arnold J. Toynbee called the *Muqaddima* (the theoretical introduction to Ibn Khaldun's historical work in which these observations are found), 'a philosophy of history which is undoubtedly the greatest work of its kind that has ever yet been created by any mind in any time or place'. Ronald Reagan was also a confirmed admirer.

Contrasting approaches to Islamic history are not limited to modern Western scholarship: traditionally, Shiites and Sunnis have viewed the unfolding of history from very different perspectives; and in recent times, 'Islamist' and 'Modernist' (or 'Reformist') interpretations of history have been promoted by their Muslim proponents. For most Sunnis (at least since the 9th century), history is no less than the implementation of God's plans on earth: the course that it has taken is thus incontrovertible. To Shiites, Islamic history has been punctuated by a series of disastrous mistakes: 'Ali should have succeeded the Prophet, but he was passed over (his six-year tenure as caliph was too little and too late); then he was martyred, as was his son Hussein; the Abbasid Revolution was meant to restore Shiism to power, but the movement's leaders changed their mind at the last minute; then the caliph al-Ma'mun sought to appoint a Shiite imam as his successor, but the latter died mysteriously (most if not all of the Twelver's imams were either imprisoned, murdered, or both); the Shiite Buyids managed to achieve power in Baghdad, but then chose to keep the Abbasid caliph on the throne; the Fatimids and Safavids did implement Shiite rule, but quickly abandoned most of their revolutionary promises; and in most parts of the Muslim (and Western) world, it is the Sunni narrative of Islamic history that has dominated. Persian nostalgia about past imperial glories combine in modern Iran with the Shiite sense of persecution to create a potent feeling of historical injustice.

Even within Sunni circles, competing approaches to Islamic history have been adopted over the centuries. The traditional Sunni approach holds that God is behind events and it is up to us to respond to the realities created in the 600–800 period, not to create new ones. Beginning in the 18th century, groups of what might now be called 'Islamists' and, from the 19th century, 'Modernists', have sponsored mutually exclusive readings of (early) Islamic history. To the Islamists, Islam's waters have been muddied over the centuries by the accumulation of unwanted accretions such as those associated with popular religious beliefs and practices. In their view, Muslims must return to their earliest sources (i.e. the Quran and *hadith*) and follow only the precepts found in them. Modernists agree with the Islamists regarding the general problem, but disagree with their literalist solution since, in their view, it puts too much emphasis on the details of history and not enough on the general 'lessons' conveyed by the Quran, Muhammad, his Companions, and their successors. The

Modernists object to the Islamists' focus on the trees rather than the wood; the latter stress that these trees were created by God and it is He who told us to focus on them.

Confusingly, both the Islamists and the Modernists are known as 'Salafis' ('those who follow [the Muslim] ancestors'). What unites them is a concern for the story of early Islamic history and an unbending conviction that it is relevant to modern Muslims. Oddly, what Salafis – particularly of the Islamist sort – have in common with Said's Orientalists is the belief that there is an original or essential Islam, which Orientalists wish to describe (and control) and which Islamists wish to reinstate. But why should things that happened over a thousand years ago be of any practical importance for people living in the 21st century? This is the question that will be addressed in the next chapter.

Chapter 6
Religious significance

'Those who do not know History are destined to repeat it'
(Edmund Burke, d. 1797) – right? Not everyone would agree:
cynics might point out that most people are not destined to
do anything noteworthy, let alone repeat history (and paying
attention in History class is unlikely to make a difference).
Moreover, in Muslim societies the idea that repeating History is
some sort of punishment for ignorance makes little sense. In fact,
there are large parts of History that are of direct and definitive
importance to the practice of Islam, and Islamic history generally
has played (and continues to play) important political roles
for Muslims and for those who interact with them. For these
reasons, Muslims over the centuries have sought to learn about
Islamic history *in order* to repeat it, or at the very least to derive
practical guidance or other benefits from its details. The political
significance of Islamic history will be discussed in the next
chapter; its religious significance will be treated in what follows.

Historical illiteracy is very common in much of the Western world.
According to a recent study, 'Fully two thirds of [American]
graduating high school seniors cannot name the half century in
which the Civil War was fought, another third cannot identify
Thomas Jefferson, [and] 65 percent think Stonewall Jackson
was a bass player for the Funkadelics'. Similarly, idealistic young
Americans (and, for that matter, non-Americans) are sometimes

seen to wear bracelets inscribed with the words 'Make Poverty History' – an entirely admirable goal except that it reflects the popular perception that History is a garbage-dump to which unwanted things should be consigned rather than a treasure-trove in which desirable things are to be found.

Other young Americans do show awareness of the past's relevance to them by wearing a different sort of bracelet, one which bears only the letters W.W.J.D. ('What Would Jesus Do?'). The point of such bracelets is to remind wearers to follow Jesus's teachings when confronted with moral dilemmas. Unsurprisingly, most Muslims do not want to know what Jesus would do; more surprising is the fact that, strictly speaking, they do not want to know what *Muhammad* would do. What Muslims want to know is what Muhammad *did* do, for which they devised the term *sunna*, a term that also covers the recorded actions and sayings of some other paradigmatic figures from early Islamic times. Superficially, *sunna* and the concept of *Imitatio Christi* ('imitating Christ', from which W.W.J.D. bracelets are descended) are comparable: in both cases, the conduct of a religion's central character is thought to have an impact on the behaviour of modern believers. Upon inspection, however, an important difference between the concepts emerges: *sunna* is completely dependent on historical knowledge – if we cannot reconstruct Muhammad's life and have no record of his utterances, then we are lost. *Imitatio Christi*, by contrast, does not depend on history; all it demands of us is that we follow Jesus's gospel of love and, more generally, that we be good. (In its original, 15th-century version, it also encouraged ascetic practices to which most young Christians no longer aspire.)

Muslims seek to emulate Muhammad for three reasons. First, the Quran tells them to do so, repeatedly and in different ways (though never unequivocally; Quran 33: 21 is the closest it gets and even this verse is far from explicit on the matter). Second, it is thought that God revealed the meaning of the Quran's verses to Muhammad as well as the verses themselves; his actions, then, are seen to reflect all that God had intended for mankind that was not stated plainly, or they are seen as the definitive interpretation of these verses. Finally, once Muslim tradition came to view Muhammad as having been infallible, the doctrine emerged that Muhammad's *sunna* must always be followed. We have seen that these ideas are associated with al-Shafi'i; as such, they were not binding before the 9th century. What is worth bearing in mind is that – as with other founding figures of great nations and religions – what Muhammad did and said is likely to have carried considerable weight from the outset. The slogan of Abbasid revolutionaries in the mid-8th century was '[We demand a return to] God's book and the *sunna* of His Prophet' – a cleverly ambiguous motto that, nonetheless, assumed Muhammad's behaviour to be high on people's agendas. The remit of the Prophet's *sunna* also included the precedent of those who knew Muhammad well and are supposed to have emulated him too, as well as the immediately succeeding generations of Muslims, all of whom are known as the '[righteous] ancestors' or *salaf*. The *salaf* as a whole can serve as exemplary models for later generations, but (again, since the 9th century) it is only Muhammad's *sunna* that shapes *shari'a*.

In recent centuries, two problems have presented themselves to Muslims who wish to adhere strictly to the *sunna*. First, as seen, the diversity of practice that resulted from Islam's spread amongst peoples of different religious and cultural backgrounds led to the assimilation of beliefs and rituals into Islam that bore little resemblance to *sunna* and, importantly, created what Salafis deem to be intolerable religious variety amongst Muslims. Second, changing historical circumstances – modernity in particular – have created situations for which there is no obvious answer in the *sunna*, as it is recorded in *hadith*s, *sira*, and other traditional sources. Salafis, in both their Islamist and Modernist forms (both of which, in turn, have their own subdivisions), sought to solve these problems by turning for guidance to the 'Islam' practised in the days of the righteous ancestors. Islamists hold that whatever was or was not done then, should or should not be done now. Modernists follow different principles: to them, God and His religion are inherently just and merciful; whatever He enjoined in the 7th century – through the Quran and *sunna* – was necessarily just and merciful. Times change, however, and some of the *sunna*'s details – while perfectly acceptable at the time of revelation – are less acceptable nowadays, for which reason such episodes must be reread in light of modern circumstances. Modernists believe in egalitarianism, democracy, and human rights, just as they believe in the Quran and in *sunna*. Hence, the Quran and *sunna* must be compatible with egalitarianism, democracy, and human rights. Modernists thus turn to Islamic history – typically *sira* and historical chronicles dealing with the *salaf* rather than *hadith*s, which are generally more categorical – to prove that such concepts have been part of Islam from the very beginning. Islamists counter by saying that it is the Quran and *sunna* that define 'justice' and not vice versa.

Put another way, both Islamists and Modernists wish to know early Islamic history in order to repeat it. That they clash on the issue of how to read early Islamic history – literally (Islamists), or each episode within its historical context (Modernists) – demonstrates how important history and its details are to [Sunni] Muslims. Most Muslims fall somewhere between the two groups and follow the *sunna* as it has been interpreted by authoritative scholars over the centuries. The centrality of *sunna* to modern Muslims is reflected in the programming schedule of the London-based 'Islam Channel' that broadcasts television shows such as *The Sunnah the Better*, which 'aims to inform and educate Muslim viewers about the importance of following the Sunnah of our prophet Muhammad'; and *The Nobles*, which explores 'the lives of the noble Companions of the Prophet Muhammad ... a generation that shined in its piety, courage, and worldly achievements'.

Wahhabism

Although the Arabian Peninsula is Islam's birthplace, from the mid-8th century, when a rebellion based in the Hijaz was quashed by the Abbasid caliph, the region was politically sidelined for a millennium, granting religious prestige to imperial rulers from the northwest or northeast who, tellingly, never considered basing themselves there. Arabia regained political prominence with the career of Muhammad ibn 'Abd al-Wahhab (d. 1792) and his followers, commonly known (by their detractors) as 'Wahhabis'; they themselves prefer the term *Muwahhidun*, 'Unitarians', on account of their uncompromising definition of monotheism. The movement is the most influential expression of Salafism of the Islamist sort, both for its role in shaping (some might say: 'creating') modern Islamism, and for disseminating *salafi* ideas widely across the Muslim world.

From his home town in the Najd province of Arabia, Ibn 'Abd al-Wahhab stressed the incompatibility with true monotheism of popular religious practices – such as visiting shrines and the tombs of saints, and adhering blindly to rituals and beliefs that had no basis in the Quran or *sunna* – and declared those who did not meet his religious standards to be infidels. As infidels, non-Wahhabi Muslims were to be subjected to *jihad*, and the shrines and tombs of the saints through whom intercession with God was sought were to be destroyed. Individually, these ideas can be traced to 7th- and 8th-century Kharijites, to 11th- to 13th-century Almoravids and Almohads (whose name, interestingly, is also derived from the Arabic *al-Muwahhidun*), and to the writings of such 14th-century scholars as Ibn Taymiyya (d. 1328) and his student Ibn Qayyim al-Jawziyya (d. 1350). Thus, like most other reformers in history, Ibn 'Abd al-Wahhab's achievement consisted of fashioning something new out of old ideas.

In the mid-18th century, the Wahhabis aligned themselves with Muhammad ibn Su'ud (later 'Saud'), the ruler of a nearby town, and for the next century and a half the Saudi family fought to extend both its rule and the Wahhabi brand of Islam throughout Arabia.

Resistance came from local inhabitants, who were horrified by the violent methods and irreverence to holy sites, and from the Ottoman sultans, who sent Egyptian forces against the movement, often achieving crushing victories against them. In the 19th century, the Saudi-Wahhabi state was also weakened by internal rivalries over succession to the imamate (amongst other issues). And yet, the numerous refutations of Wahhabi doctrine that were produced all over the Muslim world in the late 19th century attest to the influence of Wahhabi ideology, and by the early 20th century the movement's political fortunes also improved: under the leadership of Imam (then 'Sultan', then 'King') 'Abd al-'Aziz Al Saud (r. 1902–53), the Saudi-Wahhabi state managed to gain control over most of the Arabian Peninsula, establishing the Kingdom of Saudi Arabia in 1932. When, in 1938, large quantities of oil were discovered in the Kingdom's territories, Wahhabi Islam secured the means by which its message could be propagated more extensively than any other interpretation of Islam. Wahhabi mosques, schools, and educational materials are increasingly ubiquitous wherever there are Muslims.

The strict enforcement of Wahhabi doctrines has in some ways been moderated by the pragmatics of ruling a complex state, by what the regime's enemies would see as the corrupting influence of sudden and fabulous wealth, and by the influx of large numbers of (mostly economic) migrants from other Muslim societies, whose Islam differs from the Wahhabi version. This (occasional) softening of Wahhabi attitudes has paved the way for close Saudi cooperation with groups that Ibn 'Abd al-Wahhab would have deemed 'infidel', such as the *salafi* Muslim Brotherhood – a relationship that since the 1950s has seen the Saudis become the Brotherhood's most generous financial backers. It is out of the Wahhabi-*salafi* matrix that Osama bin Laden emerged, though the precise nature of his relationship with Wahhabism is disputed. Wahhabism might also contribute to our understanding of the gap that currently separates Muslim societies from Judeo-Christian, Western ones (but you will have to wait for the book's Conclusions to find out how).

Generally speaking, Shiism has also been shaped by history, but in different ways and to a different extent. From the 9th to late 18th centuries, Twelver Shiites tended towards quietism while other Shiites (most famously the Ismailis) pursued political power in the name of living imams. These days, it is the Twelvers, centred on the Islamic Republic of Iran, who represent Shiite activism (note the sword at the centre of the Iranian flag, and the fact that the state came to power through a revolution in 1979), whereas it is the Ismailis who are mostly quietist.

This shift in the Twelvers' attitude to political power is related to Shiite approaches to early Islamic history. In the late 17th century, in the absence of strong rulers in Safavid lands, Shiite *'ulama'* acquired a large measure of influence over state affairs. With the fall of the Safavids in the 18th century, a debate between two branches of Shiism ensued: the *akhbari*s held that until the twelfth imam returns, Muslims are to follow the Quran and the *sunna*, which to them included the precedents set by Muhammad and the recognized Shiite imams (as recorded in Shiite *hadith*s). For them, therefore, the history that describes the statements and actions of Shiite authorities (the 'Shiite *salaf*' as it were) is of direct relevance to the practice of Islam. Their opponents were the *usuli*s, who argued that current Shiite practice must rely on the *ijtihad* (personal interpretation of Islamic law) of leading *'ulama'*. By the end of the 18th century, the *usuli*s had won the debate, and in many ways it is *usuli* Shiism that accounts for the Iranian Revloution: the proliferation of qualified practitioners of *ijtihad* (*mujtahid*s) led to the creation of a clerical hierarchy at the top of which are the Grand Ayatollahs, one of whom – Ayatollah Khomeini – was the Revolution's dominant figure. The Revolution's unofficial manifesto, Khomeini's book *Islamic Government: The Guardianship of Jurists*, argues that to ensure that Muslims practise authentic Islam, they must live in an Islamic state, run by a leading *mujtahid*-jurist (*faqih*). After the Revolution's success, Ayatollah Khomeini became the first such ruler.

The reliance on living *mujtahid*s necessarily reduces the impact of *sunna* on Shiite Islam, and the general perception amongst Shiites that the course of history has been misguided ever since 'Ali was passed over in the succession dispute following Muhammad's death, have decreased Islamic history's role in determining Shiite practice. That said, there are two ways in which Shiism and History have combined to create practices that are unique (at least originally) to Shiite Islam: *Ta'ziya* passion-plays and martyrdom operations.

According to all Shiites, 'Ali's second son, Hussein, was the third imam in line to succeed Muhammad (preceded by 'Ali and his oldest son Hasan). When the Umayyads came to power in 661, it became increasingly clear that Hussein was unlikely to rule as imam, and in 680, together with his supporters, he launched a rebellion against the Umayyad caliph Yazid. This was brutally quashed at Karbala on the tenth day of the first month of the Muslim calendar, which until then had been observed as a voluntary fast day (corresponding to the Jewish Yom Kippur, also observed on the tenth of the first month). To commemorate Hussein's martyrdom at Yazid's hands, Shiites have marked this anniversary by staging passion-plays (*ta'ziya*) in which Hussein's suffering and murder are re-enacted. The *ta'ziya* is a popular ritual, widespread wherever there are Shiite communities, and the events present locals with the opportunity to reflect on religious and moral issues, and in some cases to level thinly veiled criticism against authorities by putting their unpopular political statements into Yazid's mouth in the play. Thus, an episode of 7th-century history has provided Shiism with one of its most distinctive rituals.

Martyrdom operations, or 'suicide missions', are theoretically prohibited in Sunni Islam. Those who die waging *jihad* will become martyrs, of course, but classical sources maintain that it is forbidden to set out with the intention of dying in battle (Quran 4: 29 being the verse adduced in support of this view).

16. *Ta'ziya* passion-play (**Karachi, Pakistan**). **The horse represents Hussein's mount**

Many Shiites disagree, and the martyrdom of Hussein (and of most other Twelver imams, for that matter) combines with the sense of victimhood discussed above to provide Shiites with a tradition that condones such practices. It is no coincidence that in Islamic history, the group most (in)famous for embarking on suicide missions were Shiites (the Ismaili 'Assassins'), nor is it a coincidence that suicide attacks in the modern era were pioneered by the Shiite group Hezbollah ('The Party of God'; its first 'martyrdom operation' took place in Beirut in 1983). The efficacy of this cheap, low-tech method of warfare brought it to the attention of Sunni Islamists, some of whom have adopted it since, but only hesitantly. The permissibility of martyrdom operations continues to be hotly debated amongst Sunni authorities.

Episodes from the biographies of the Prophet and the *salaf* (and, for Shiites, the imams) have inspired the behaviour of religiously minded Muslims even when not invoked as part of *shari'a*. The birth of Islam, for instance, has been the paradigm for religious revolutionaries throughout Islamic history. Thus, the Kharijites argued that it is imperative to depart from lands under illegitimate (i.e., non-Kharijite) rule, a departure they termed *hijra*, following the Prophet's precedent of immigrating from pagan Mecca to Medina. The Abbasid and Fatimid revolutions acted out *hijra*s of their own: the former departed from 'the centre' for Khurasan, only to return to the centre to defeat their foes (as Muhammad did); the latter emigrated to Yemen and North Africa before returning eastwards to Egypt as successful conquerors. More striking are those Muslim reformers and political activists (usually in Africa) who closely patterned their movements on the Prophet's life. Usman dan Fodio (1754–1817), for instance, led his followers out of their home town (a *hijra*) and launched a *jihad* in what is modern Nigeria against the local Muslims in Hausaland whose practice of Islam was deemed to be unacceptable (due to its accommodation of pre-Islamic rituals). He incited his followers to *jihad* using rhyming verse (cf. the Quran, which is mostly in rhymed prose), and his successors were called 'caliphs'. The Mahdi of Sudan in the late 19th century is another example of this: he also went on a *hijra*, his supporters were called '*ansar*' (this having been the term for Muhammad's supporters in Medina), and he too was succeeded by a 'caliph'.

Another example of early Islamic history's informal influence on Muslims comes from an online *fatwa* issued by Shaykh Yusuf al-Qaradawi (b. 1926). When asked whether Muslims should boycott Israeli goods, he replied:

> Arabs and Muslims must boycott all companies that are biased towards Zionism…The boycott is a very sharp weapon, used in the past and recently. It was used by the pagans in Mecca against the Prophet Muhammad (peace and blessings be upon him) and his Companions. It caused great harm to them; they even had to eat leaves. It was also used by Companions of the Prophet (peace and blessings be upon him) to fight against the pagans in Medina.

Al-Qaradawi's answer is not that boycotts are an obligatory part of the *sunna* but that historically they have proven to be effective. The point here is that the history he draws on is from the Prophet's biography, both because it is the first port of call for Sunni authorities who seek traditional answers to modern questions, and for its wide resonance. In a similar vein, when the immensely influential Islamist Sayyid Qutb sought to delegitimize the Muslim authorities and societies of his time, he referred to them as representing a *jahiliyya*, deliberately echoing the 'age of ignorance' that spawned Muhammad's mission and the rise of Islam.

In some of these cases, it is difficult to distinguish between 'religious' and 'political' significance of Islamic history since any political relevance borne by the careers of Muhammad and the *salaf* is directly related to their religious prestige amongst religious people. There are, however, ways in which Islamic history can be used by those with few religious qualifications or pretensions to influence Muslims who are uninterested in religion (or those who are not Muslims at all), as we will now see.

Chapter 7
Political significance

It is often stated that one of the most significant differences between the Judeo-Christian West and Islam is that the latter has no tradition of separating 'Church' from 'State'. Although many books treat such issues, this is not one of them. All that is to be said here is that things are not so simple: from the 10th century (if not earlier), there was a *de facto* distinction between the administrations of religious affairs, on the one hand, and of governmental affairs, on the other, with different groups claiming and exercising authority over each sphere. The two spheres might occasionally overlap – waging *jihad* is relevant to both religion and government – but they are generally distinguishable nonetheless. In fact, it is this separation of 'religion' and 'politics' that Islamists seek to undo, and it is this separation that has dictated this book's layout: the previous chapter dealt with Islamic history's influence on religious affairs; the present chapter deals with its influence on politics.

All people consider their relationship to the past (even if only to reject it), and Muslims are no exception: when Osama bin Laden compared the US-led invasion of Iraq to the Mongol conquest of the region in the 1250s, he was striking an historical chord that has rung continuously over the past 750 years. The Mongol destruction of the Abbasid caliphate has endured in the *umma*'s collective memory just as the Battle of Hastings (1066) survives amongst the British: it is hardly surprising that people remember significant events. What sets apart the status of Islamic history amongst Muslims is that it is not just the grand themes and pivotal moments of history but also many of its (often random) details that are familiar and evocative to Muslims everywhere. Moreover, the esteem in which history is held in Muslim societies has even led to its deployment in political contexts in which the intended audience is non-Muslim, all of which will be demonstrated below.

Not all periods and regions of Islamic history have equal resonance amongst Muslims. As a general rule, the earlier an episode, the more likely it is to be known widely, and accounts of Muhammad, his Companions, and the early Conquests are particularly popular. Accordingly, almost without exception, the entire historical repository on which Muslims have drawn for political purposes consists of episodes from the 600–800, 800–1100, and 1100–1500 periods. This is because, until recently, whenever Islam spread to a new region, the historical record that was imported together with the religion tended to become static, with subsequent chapters in the story being comprised of local events rather than those taking place elsewhere. In pre-modern times, the *hajj* allowed Muslims from all over to update each other about developments in distant lands, but it is only modern technology that has redefined the relationship between Muslim societies and post-1500 history, bringing recent events to the attention of Muslims everywhere.

Another general rule is that historical events that took place in central Islamic lands have wider circulation than those from peripheral ones. Consider the following example. In a contentious part of the Islamic world, a large wall of separation has been constructed by one of the governments in order to impose its own vision of international boundaries on a disputed territory. Opponents of the 2,700-kilometre barrier call it the 'Wall of Shame' and many of the indigenous people who live beyond the wall have refugee status. The wall referred to here runs through the western Sahara and was built in the 1980s by the Moroccan government, who prefer to call it 'the Berm' (were you thinking of some other wall?). That fact that this wall is relatively unknown, while another, much shorter wall in Israel–Palestine has become infamous, illustrates the imbalance between different regions and periods of the Islamic world: some regions have always had what appears to be disproportionate influence on collective consciousness while other regions can fade rather quickly out of focus. Morocco was late to be incorporated into the caliphate and early to break away from it, unlike the Muslim lands of the Near East, wherefrom power and influence emanated and where it remained for centuries thereafter. Even amongst the central Islamic lands, the Holy Land has acquired an exceptional degree of significance, combining as it does historical episodes from the *Sira*, the early Conquests, and caliphal history; touching on interfaith polemics; and being the subject of a considerable corpus of religious literature over the ages.

Islamic history's significance may be discerned in the political language employed from the rise of Islam until modern times. In some cases, it could be argued that the remarkable similarity between classical and modern forms of Arabic accounts for the use of 'historical' vocabulary in modern contexts. For instance, the term *fida'i* ('one who sacrifices himself for another') was first used in a political sense early on in the 1100–1500 period with reference to the Ismaili Assassins, and it resurfaces in its plural form, *fedayeen*, in the mid-20th century amongst Iranians, Palestinians, Egyptians, and Iraqis. In other cases, however, the use of historically loaded terminology is unmistakably conscious: Berber revolts against the early conquerors of North Africa were referred to as *Ridda* (echoing the *Ridda* wars that followed Muhammad's death), just as the religious reformers encountered in the previous chapter presented their careers in terms taken from the *Sira*. Similarly, modern Muslim states – especially Egypt under Gamal Abdel Nasser (d. 1970), Anwar al-Sadat (d. 1981),

121

and Hosni Mubarak (b. 1928) – have attempted to discredit Islamist opponents to their rule by labelling them 'Kharijites', thereby associating these groups with harmful disunity (*fitna*) such as that attributed to the Kharijites of early Islam.

Rivalries in modern Muslim societies have also been framed in terms of traditional conflicts in Islamic history. Two groups in 19th-century Sudan that competed for local water resources pitted themselves against each other by claiming descent from the Umayyads and Abbasids respectively. And when, from the 17th to the 20th centuries, rival factions of Ottoman Palestine and Lebanon competed for influence, the two sides described themselves as 'Qays' and 'Yaman'. These names are said to derive from pre-Islamic times, when the inhabitants of northern Arabia (the Qays) were joined by emigrants from the south (or Yemen, hence 'Yaman'), creating two large confederations of Arabian tribes. The distinctions are thought to have been reformulated in the mid-7th century, when members of both tribal groups settled in garrison towns in the Near East and retraced their lineages to reflect the new settlement patterns and alliances that resulted from the upheaval to Arabian society brought about by the Conquests. From c. 700, once the dust of the second Civil War (680–92) had settled, two distinct 'Qays' and 'Yaman' factions had emerged whose rivalry would dominate the politics of the Umayyad caliphate. Historians cannot agree on the origins, nature, or significance of the rivalry; by contrast, for inhabitants of Palestine and Lebanon in the recent past, the historical reference was nonchalant and effortless.

Obviously, the significance of drawing on History's terminology in political contexts might be somewhat limited: when English-speakers refer to childbirth by 'Caesarean section', they are not usually making a point about Roman history and legends about Julius Caesar; and when they speak of doing something 'vicariously', they tend not to have the intricacies of church structures in mind. It is therefore important to note that there are contemporary political issues in which Islamic history has come to play conscious, deliberate roles, of two sorts. In some instances, as a means to rally the *umma* as a whole behind a political cause; in others, to clarify a ruler's perspective on a political issue and hint at how he expects it to be resolved, by referring to episodes of Islamic history whose outcome is of course known. Two case studies of relevance to modern readers will suffice to demonstrate this in action: the ongoing Israel–Palestine conflict and the Iran–Iraq war (1980–8).

Israel–Palestine

Islamic history wields more political influence over this issue than over any other for two reasons that are consistent with the general rules mentioned above. First, the modern conflict can easily be related to episodes that are detailed in the *Sira*, in which Muhammad's relations with the Jews are central to his career in Medina (and second in importance only to his relations with the Meccans). Accordingly, the Prophet's biography (coloured by several hundred relevant *hadith*s) can be adduced to demonstrate that 'the Jews' are untrustworthy, deceitful, haughty, conniving, and deserving of Muslim retribution. Conveniently, 'the Jews' is the most common label for 'Israelis' in most Muslim media. Thus, members of Hezbollah have been heard to chant 'Khaybar, Khaybar O Jews, Muhammad's army will return [bearing bad news]' (it rhymes in Arabic), referring to Muhammad's defeat of the Jews of the Khaybar oasis in 628 and, crucially, linking modern Israelis with the Jews of Muhammad's day. Jews in Israel have even been cast in the role of Muhammad's Meccan enemies (whose actual descendants cannot embody opposition to the *umma* since, as Muslims, they are part of it). Thus, the Egyptian attack on the Israeli Bar-Lev Line (a chain of fortifications along the Suez Canal) in 1973 was code-named 'Operation Badr', referring to Muhammad's defeat of the *Meccans* at Badr in 624. Finally, an example of a Muslim leader's reference to Islamic history as an indication of his political intentions comes from Yasser Arafat's repeated insistence that any peace accord with Israel is a 'Hudaybiyya Treaty'. Observers ignorant of Islamic history would have missed the implication that, as with Muhammad's deal with the Meccans at Hudaybiyya in 628, the peace with Israel is only a ten-year truce that can be broken at the slightest provocation (Muhammad ended the treaty in 629).

Second, Palestine has been at the centre of a number of pivotal episodes in Islamic history, most of which turn on the region's holiness. According to traditional sources, Muslims initially prayed facing Jerusalem, and it is only after 624 that the direction of prayer (*qibla*) was changed to Mecca. Early Arabic sources also hold that 'Abd al-Malik built the Dome of the Rock in an attempt to divert the *hajj* from Mecca (where his chief political rival was based) to Jerusalem, for which religious authorities at the time are said to have stressed Jerusalem's equivalence with Mecca and even superiority to it. Modern scholars point out that the conquest of Jerusalem decades earlier had messianic overtones for contemporary Jews (and, according to particularly adventurous scholars, for Muslims too). That the Byzantines and, famously, the Crusaders attempted with varying degrees of success to retake Jerusalem and the Holy Land served to reinforce the importance of the region and the need to fight for it: the Crusades spawned a genre of Muslim literature that extolled Jerusalem's virtues, and underlined the *umma*'s responsibility to protect it from infidel aggression.

Predictably, historical victories over Palestine's invaders have been evoked by politicians seeking to present themselves as popular Muslim heroes: both the Syrian president Hafez al-Assad (r. 1971–2000) and the Iraqi president Saddam Hussein (r. 1979–2003) built monuments to Saladin in their capitals.

Saddam, moreover, publicly compared himself to both Saladin and Nebuchadnezzar, the former having been a fellow native of Tikrit (north of Baghdad), and famous for evicting the Crusaders

17. Saddam Hussein and Nebuchadnezzar (r. 605–562 BCE)

18. Statue of Saladin (Damascus, Syria)

from the Holy Land; the latter having been a fellow ruler of Iraq (or 'Babylonia'), and famous for evicting the Jews from the Holy Land in ancient times. Saddam's point was clear: he is the ruler who will come to the aid of Muslims in Palestine by defeating the Jews and thereby restoring the land to Muslim rule. 'The Jews' for their part have accordingly become 'the Crusaders' in political speeches, public debates, and even in children's schoolbooks in some parts of the Muslim world. Thus, the Israeli siege of Beirut in 1982 was compared in local media to the Crusaders' siege of Acre in 1189–91: in this example (which is but one amongst many) it is not just that Muslims made the obvious, superficial comparison between modern infidel invaders of Palestine and medieval ones, but that a relatively obscure episode of medieval history was casually adduced and deemed generally intelligible. The current Western preoccupation with the Israel–Palestine conflict (which largely ignores other, more violent or costly, conflicts) is principally an acknowledgement of the issue's importance to Muslims.

The Iran–Iraq War

Saddam Hussein put Islamic history to its most extensive political use during the Iran–Iraq war, to which Ayatollah Khomeini and the Iranians responded with history lessons of their own. Both sides viewed Islamic history as a sharp propaganda tool, through which military and popular support for their campaigns could be garnered, both within Iran and Iraq, and amongst the *umma* at large.

Expectedly, Iran's Shiites focused on the Battle of Karbala, the martyrdom of 'Ali's son Hussein, and the tyranny of the Umayyad caliph Yazid, who was represented in this context by the Iraqi leader. It is very likely that such historical references directly inspired Iranian troops, who were 'martyred' in very large numbers during the war (Iranian casualties were in excess of one million killed or wounded). No fewer than ten Iranian military operations were dubbed 'Operation Karbala', though it is also worth noting that here too the Palestine issue was seen to be worth deploying: an Iranian advance towards Basra was labelled 'Operation Khaybar' and an early Iranian war slogan proclaimed that 'The Road to Jerusalem goes through Baghdad'.

Even before the war, Saddam's antipathy towards Iran and its peoples was expressed in public statements about the role of 'Persians' in the murders of the second, third, and fourth Rightly Guided caliphs. On the eve of the Iran–Iraq war and throughout its course, the Iranians were often referred to as 'the *furs*', this being the term used in Islamic history for the pre-Islamic Persians who were conquered by the *umma* in the 7th century. The pivotal battle in the conquest of Iran took place at al-Qadisiyya in 637, and Saddam thus called the entire conflict 'Saddam's Qadisiyya', stressing the victory of Arabs (Iraq) over Persians (Iran). This historical reference was of such significance that the Iranian leaders countered by confirming that the Iran–Iraq war *was* in fact another Qadisiyya, representing as it does a Muslim (Iranian) victory over infidel forces (the secular Iraqi government). It is, however, the Iraqis and other Sunnis in the region who have consistently taken pride in the victory at al-Qadisiyya, with universities in Jordan and Iraq and football clubs in Kuwait and Saudi Arabia being named after the battle. Modern Iranian football teams have also been inspired by Islamic history: the Meshhed-based 'Abu Muslim' club takes its name from the leading architect of the Abbasid Revolution (747–50).

Here, as in the Israel–Palestine case, the point is that it is not only the big moments of history on which Muslims draw, but also the names of people, towns, battles, and other events that took place some 13 centuries ago. The fact that political uses of Islamic history might consist of little more than a cursory allusion to an historical episode from the early centuries and central lands of Islam demonstrates how resonant Islamic history is even to the general public, large parts of which might be undereducated or even illiterate. Amongst Muslim peoples, History occupies society's cafés and alleyways as well as its ivory towers.

Nationalism and Islamic history

The religious and political significance of Islamic history, coupled with emerging ideas about nationalism, identity, and history that were imported to the Muslim world from the West in the 19th century, combined to create distinctively 'ethnic' narratives. Some of these employed Islamic history directly, while others skewed its traditional story and message. Thus, the 'nationalistic' Iraqi reading of Islamic history promoted during the Iran–Iraq war, which consciously pitted Arab heroes against Persian villains, was indebted to an approach to history that was adopted by Arab, Persian, and Turkish nationalists long before the 1980s.

Muhammad is recorded as having said, 'Love of one's country is an article of Faith', but in practice loyalty to one's nation often clashed with loyalty to the *umma*. On the one hand, nationalistic movements adopted 'Islamic' ideas: Arab nationalists, for instance, chose not to belong to an Arab 'nation' (*sha'b*) but to an Arab *umma*. On the other hand, the conscious construction of new identities demanded that history itself be pressed into a nation's service – especially amongst peoples for whom history had traditionally played a formative role in defining one's place in the world. Thus, rather than being abandoned by nationalists, Islamic history was reinterpreted to suit new narratives and new political purposes.

Both because of potential conflicts of interest between nationality and Islamic identity, and because those Arabs, Persians, and Turks who promoted nationalistic movements were often secular Muslims or not Muslim at all, traditional Islamic versions of history gave way to historical perspectives that transcended religion: sources of inspiration and national pride were sought in Islamic figures and also in pre-Islamic ones, the latter of whom might have been maligned in traditional sources. In this way, Nebuchadnezzar and the Egyptian Pharaohs became Arab heroes rather than villains of Near Eastern monotheists; Turks proudly traced their ancestry back to ancient (non-monotheistic) peoples such as the Hittites and Sumerians; the Lebanese reclaimed their Phoenician heritage (real or imagined); and Palestinians came to remember that they are descended from Canaanites (which handily allowed them to stake a pre-Israelite claim to possession of the Holy Land).

Not only were un-Islamic (and even anti-Islamic) historical figures aggrandized by nationalists, but Islamic history itself came to be refracted through new lenses. Arab nationalists, for instance, consciously glorified the *jahiliyya* (the term for pre-Islamic Arabian society that Islamists used as a byword for ungodliness and immorality). Similarly, the reputation of the Umayyad caliphs, whose general impiety and usurpation of the caliphal office was written into the traditional story of Islamic history by Abbasid-era scholars and those who relied on them, was rehabilitated by Pan-Arabists. According to one Syrian scholar writing in the 1940s, Damascus under the Umayyads was:

> the home of kings and caliphs...the most important capital of the ancient world, the seat of civilization and culture, the administrative centre of a great empire and of a great army. [The Umayyad period was] when poetry, literature and art, the leadership of thought, science, war and administration, converged on the banks of its small rivers; and when Damascus was the world and the world was Damascus.

Traditional Muslims might not recognize this as an acceptable version of history, but the sort of political uses to which history is put in this instance should be more familiar to them.

Islamic history and Western societies

Islamic history is clearly of direct religious and political relevance to Muslims everywhere, whether they are traditional Sunnis,

Islamist Salafis, Modernist Salafis, Shiites, or others. In recent decades, there have also been attempts (by Westerners as well as Muslims) to share some of Islamic history's lessons with non-Muslims in the West, in order to further political agendas.

This trend is best represented by the myth and counter-myth of the Golden Age of Spain (hereafter: GAS). The argument goes that in Andalusia, under Islamic rule, Muslims, Christians, and Jews lived in an interfaith utopia where they flourished under the stable protection of Muslim rule. The late 19th-century German Jewish scholars who came up with this idea used it to chastise their local, supposedly enlightened, colleagues for not affording German Jews the same level of equality that (even) pre-modern Muslims did. More recently, the GAS idea has been used by anti-Zionists and Islamists to argue that the founding of the State of Israel is to blame for the present conflict in the region; previously, they say, Muslims and Jews had coexisted in peace and harmony and it is the Zionist movement that upset such a favourable status quo. For the anti-Zionists, Israel must be disbanded so that harmony can be restored to the region; for the Islamists, all non-Muslims should live under Muslim rule as it is only under Islam that all faiths can live in peace.

The GAS argument provoked an equally simplistic response by those (often Jews forced out of Muslim lands in the past century) who created a counter-myth, according to which Jews and Christians have consistently been maltreated by Islam and Muslims throughout history, in Spain and elsewhere too. Non-Muslims under Islam were second-class citizens, exposed to the whims of fanatical rulers who spread Islam by the sword and haphazardly looted the properties of their infidel subjects. Both the GAS and anti-GAS arguments are hopelessly injudicious on numerous counts. On the one hand, it is difficult to argue that there really was an interfaith utopia in Andalusia – even Maimonides (1135–1204), the poster-boy for interfaith programmes and Abrahamic unity, was forced to flee Almohad

Spain, just as many Jews sought refuge from Almoravid violence in towns re-conquered by the Christians in the late 11th century. Although the culture produced by non-Muslims in Andalusia is impressive in both quantity and quality, the use to which the GAS idea is put concerns extreme political tolerance, and such conditions rarely existed in Andalusia (with the possible exception of Cordoba in the mid to late 10th century). On the other hand, it is also inaccurate to speak of non-Muslims as second-class citizens. Even disregarding the anachronism, it is clear that in most Muslim societies in history, some Christians and Jews have managed to rise to high administrative positions, while some of their Muslim neighbours struggled to make ends meet.

What is important here is not the historicity of these theories but the fact that they are deployed by and for Westerners at all. Though Islamic history obviously has little religious significance for non-Muslims (at least in the absence of a worldwide caliphate), its political significance is beginning to be felt, a point to which we will return in the following chapter.

Conclusions

Non-Arabian converts to Islam in the first Islamic century might have found the Arabian character of the religion somewhat alien, but those who converted since Abbasid times have been seamlessly absorbed into the religion, and can immediately plug their experiences, cultures, and pasts into an ever-growing network of Muslim societies. Moreover, as the foregoing two chapters have shown, they can adopt and tap into a ready-made, rich, and well-defined historical repository in the pursuit of both religious and political aims.

For these reasons, Islamic history is perhaps the only religious tradition whose formative and classical history is not specific to a nationality or ethnicity. Few people choose to adopt Judaism at all (let alone its history), and although there are many who have adopted Christianity, the link between the Christian tradition and a distinct body of history is tenuous. Even those episodes of Christian history that have retained significance into modern times – such as the Crusades – have more resonance for some Christians (e.g. Western Europeans) than for others (e.g. South Americans). George W. Bush famously said, 'I think we agree: the past is over'; it is but one statement of his amongst many with which most Muslims would take real issue.

Conclusion

I owe the reader some answers to a question posed eight chapters ago: Why, despite sharing common roots in Semitic monotheism of the Near East, do Muslim societies and Western ones appear to be headed for a clash? This question makes assumptions to which some readers will object. They might say that there *is* no such tension between Muslims and Westerners; or that there is no such thing as 'Muslims' or 'Westerners' at all – merely individuals or individual societies that should not be grouped together under generalized rubrics; or that the very question betrays cultural bias – pro- or anti-Western, pro- or anti-Muslim – or naïveté. (Those readers will almost certainly dislike what follows.) Though such objections are reasonable, and the diversity of Muslim societies has been a dominant theme of this book, it should be recognized that to answer general questions we occasionally must revert to (admittedly imperfect) generalizations. Furthermore, there are people in prominent positions in both Muslim and Western societies who think that a clash either has already happened, is happening, or will inevitably happen between 'Islam' and 'the West'. Surely the public statements of some leaders on both sides, and in some cases their actions on the ground, leave no doubt as to the legitimacy of this book's big question. How can Islamic history help answer it?

Different chapters of this book provide answers of their own. Chapters 1 to 3 offer four plausible answers, focusing on geography, 'external' cultural influences, the track-record of Muslim–Western relations, and the political circumstances of Islam's formation. The geographical environment in which Islamic history unfolded shaped Muslim societies in very particular ways. The Great Arid Zone presented Muslims with harsh realities that determined everything from urban planning to the emergence and survival of sectarian movements. That Muslim lands had active frontiers with Africa, Europe, Central Asia, and South Asia meant that Muslim societies were exposed to diverse civilizations and influences in addition to Near Eastern monotheism. Our encounter with the peoples of Islamic history also highlighted the decisive influences that Persians and Turks have exerted over Muslim societies, from the late 8th century onwards. 'Islam' and 'the West' may have begun from similar starting points, but their 'roads diverged in a wood' fairly quickly, and that indeed has made all the difference.

Another history-based answer is that 'Muslim' engagement with 'Western' culture, as represented by Europe for geographical reasons, has been dominated by antagonism, of which current tensions are either a continuation or a reflex. Early rivalries with Byzantium, followed by wars against Christian states in the Mediterranean, the Crusades, *Reconquista*, the Ottoman expansion into and withdrawal from Europe, and, finally, colonialism, have naturally bred mistrust between 'Muslims' and 'Westerners'. This series of rivalries and the memories – both recent and distant – of Western enmity, oppression, and colonization that result from it, may discourage modern Muslims from 'investing' in Western culture. This lack of investment has had significant consequences: a recent book on the 100 'most influential Muslims in history' includes only one Western Muslim – Malcolm X – who can hardly be taken as a success-story for Muslim–Western cooperation. In fact, for his political views, Malcolm X might not be considered a hero by many in the West;

for his association with the 'Nation of Islam', he might not be considered a Muslim by many in the Islamic world. This may be something of a vicious cycle, as the more mutual scepticism exists between the two sides, the less likely Muslims will be to 'invest' fully in Western culture. The list of Muslim heroes will thus continue to be dominated by pre-modern, non-Western figures who are celebrated *only* by Muslims; Muslim feelings of alienation from non-Muslim societies will be nurtured and perpetuated accordingly. On a more optimistic note, this vicious cycle's fragility has been exposed by Europe's other non-Christian minority, the Jews. Although Christian Europe has a long history of persecuting Jews and, until recently, extreme inhospitality towards them, Europe's Jews produced Einstein, Freud, Marx, and numerous others who are revered by Jewish and non-Jewish Europeans alike. Thus, given time and favourable circumstances, Western Muslims are likely to produce crossover-heroes of their own.

The story of Islamic history also alerts us to a fundamental difference between the formation of Islamic institutions, on the one hand, and of Jewish and Christian ones, on the other. Although Muhammad and his Companions faced two decades of hardship and even persecution, the Prophet died as the head of his community, having defeated his Meccan enemies and converted the tribes of Arabia to Islam. Over the following centuries, Islamic rule spread while the classical doctrines, law-books, and institutions of Islam were being developed, usually with state patronage and from a position of political strength. By contrast, Moses never made it into the Holy Land and Jesus died on the Cross. Until Constantine adopted Christianity as the official faith of the eastern Roman empire in the 4th century CE, Christians had been a persecuted minority for centuries (during which, crucially, the Gospels were written and the founding fathers of the religion lived). Judaism is the product of sources (the *Mishna* and *Talmud*s) written under 'foreign' rule, following the destruction of the Second Temple (c. 70 CE). Thus, Judaism and Christianity were born (or, in Judaism's case, crystallized) during periods of political weakness and without royal patronage or support. Although first Christians and later Jews subsequently attained political muscle of their own, Jewish and Christian sources take for granted the practicalities of living under the rule of others, based on experiences acquired during the 'classical' periods of these two religions. By contrast, the most important works of Islamic law, especially those composed in the 800–1100 period, usually refer back to events that took place in the 600–800 period. The Muslim jurists thus do not conceive of the possibility of living under 'foreign' rule (a situation that presented itself only in the mid-11th century). There are, of course, later sources written under Mongol, Crusader, or Iberian Christian rule, which take changing political circumstances into account; and some of these sources have proven to be popular and influential. (Many of these sources advise Muslims living under foreign rule to perform a *hijra* to Muslim lands, where the practice of Islam is not compromised.) The point is that the majority of Islamic legal sources, and the earliest and most prestigious of them, advise Muslims to practise their faith with the assertiveness of a dominant religious culture. Therefore, what many Westerners might perceive amongst practising Muslims to be an intransigence that hinders neighbourly relations, or a general unwillingness to adapt their faith to the current cultures of non-Muslim countries, may be explained with reference to the course of Islamic history.

Chapters 4 and 5 provide us with two further answers, coming from opposite ends of the historiographical spectrum. The traditional Muslim approach to Islamic history holds that Islam is different either because it is the Jews and Christians who distorted God's original faith, or because Islam emerged fully formed from the Arabian Peninsula, based on revelations received by a prophet who was isolated from the influence of Late Antiquity in the Near East. Accordingly, Islam is distinct from Judeo-Christian culture because of its unique Arabian context; any comparison between the two (or three) religious traditions is to be rejected as a misguided Orientalist enterprise. A diametrically opposed answer comes from Wansborough, who, in *The Sectarian Milieu*, argued that the Arab conquerors of Iraq in the 8th century *consciously* distinguished themselves from Jews and Christians, creating a specifically Arabian religion (with a new calendar, sanctuary, and theological system) in contradistinction to the pre-existing local ones. Unlike the early Christians, who saw themselves as the new (or real) Jews, the early Muslims, in Wansborough's view, saw themselves as the new *non*-Jews or *non*-Christians.

Chapters 6 and 7 illustrated the stark contrast between the Islamic world's attachment to history and the West's relative amnesia with regard to its own, which leads us to another answer to our question. The case could be made that it is not the Muslims who strayed from the path of Near Eastern monotheism, but rather the Westerners who did so. During the Renaissance, Reformation, and Enlightenment, the Judeo-Christian West made a clean break with the past (or, more precisely, with their real past in favour of a legendary Classical one). Who, after all, would want to revive a period known as the 'Dark Ages'? Accordingly, it is Islam rather than the West that is the true heir to Judeo-Christian civilization.

For many analysts, this is precisely the point: the answer to our big question comes not from something that happened in Islamic history but from things that did not happen, namely a Renaissance or Reformation, which would allow Muslims to emerge from what is perceived to be the backwardness of 'medieval' conservatism. This is a simple solution to a complex problem. Much depends, of course, on what 'Renaissance' and 'Reformation' are taken to mean. If a Renaissance is literally a 'rebirth' of Classical civilization, then one may say that Muslims experienced one many centuries before Europe did, in 9th-century Baghdad. If, on the other hand, we take the Renaissance to refer to the revival of *any* past period deemed to be culturally glorious, then it may be said that this is precisely what Islamists have advocated for centuries: it's just that the 'classical period' that they seek to resurrect is that of Muhammad and his Companions.

Pundits are also heard to argue that Muslim societies would engage more favourably with 'the West' if only they were to experience an Islamic version of the Protestant Reformation of the Catholic Church (c. 1517–1648). The Reformation is credited with loosening the Church's grip on society and paving the way for freedom of conscience in Western Christendom, both of which led to the elevation of 'moral values' above all else. An Islamic Reformation, so the argument runs, would imbue Muslim societies with ideas of pluralism, religious tolerance, and intellectual and cultural freedom, all of which would bring Islam into line with the rest of the 'modern' world. There are two problems with this answer. First, it ignores the fact that the Protestant Reformation was followed by over a century of violence and the irreversible fragmentation of Christian society. Nobody could reasonably propose that Muslims, for whom the *umma*'s unity and the avoidance of communal strife (*fitna*) are of central importance, should risk bringing upheaval upon themselves so that non-Muslim Westerners might feel more comfortable in their dealings with them. Second, it could be argued that Muslims *have* had a Reformation in the form of Wahhabism. The Wahhabis and Protestants both sought to purge the True Faith of accretions such as the widespread devotion to saints (in both cases) or the veneration of Mary (in the Christian case). Likewise, just as Martin Luther was influenced by earlier thinkers such as John Wycliffe and Jan Hus, so Muhammad ibn 'Abd al-Wahhab benefited from the writings of Ibn Taymiyya and Ibn Qayyim al-Jawziyya. Thus, Muslims have had their Reformation, but some in the West would prefer it to have taken a different form and produced different results. To the extent that Wahhabism and other forms of Salafism continue to compete with traditional Sunni, Sufi, and Shiite interpretations of Islam, it may well be the case that we have yet to witness the Islamic Reformation's dénouement.

At the beginning of this book it was noted that 'Islam matters'. I hope to have shown that Islamic *history* 'matters' too. We have seen some of the many ways in which Islamic history shapes politics and religion in the Muslim world, and have considered its contribution to our understanding of the relationship between the Islamic world and the modern, 'Judeo-Christian' West. It should be stressed in this context that Islamic history is not the only thing that matters – far from it. Analysts who apply themselves to the issue of Muslim–Western relations (from either side or from neither) are generally aware that Muslims and Westerners share life's most basic concerns and worries – we all want peace, health, prosperity, respect, and a better future, and we fear having to live in the absence of these things. Muslim–Western interactions thus tend to be measured and interpreted in terms of geopolitics, economics, and other 'usual' factors, with tensions between the two being blamed on imbalances in the accessibility of necessary resources. What this book has attempted to show is that a frequently overlooked piece of the puzzle is Islamic history. Non-Muslims in the West are unaware of this point as history plays a relatively minor role in their own societies. Whether or not readers of this book continue to ignore their own history, it is hoped they have come to appreciate *Islamic* history's importance – not only to Muslims, but also to those who seek to engage with them, and to understand Islam and Muslims on their own terms.

References and further reading

Introduction

X. de Planhol, *The World of Islam* (New York, 1959), a translation of *Le Monde islamique: essai de géographie réligieuse* (Paris, 1957).

Chapter 1

General works:

J. L. Esposito (ed.), *The Oxford History of Islam* (Oxford, 1999).

F. Robinson (ed.), *The Cambridge Illustrated History of the Islamic World* (Cambridge, 1996).

W. C. Brice and H. Kennedy, *An Historical Atlas of Islam* (Leiden, 2001).

Introductory surveys:

J. Berkey, *The Formation of Islam: Religion and Society in the Near East, 600–1800* (Cambridge, 2003).

A. Hourani, *A History of the Arab Peoples* (London, 1991).

B. Lewis, *The Arabs in History* (London, 1950, and numerous reprints).

Detailed analyses:

M. G. S. Hodgson, *The Venture of Islam: Conscience and History in a World Civilization* (Chicago, 1974).

I. M. Lapidus, *A History of Islamic Societies* (Cambridge, 1988).

Camels and Islamic civilization:

R. Bulliet, *The Camel and the Wheel* (Cambridge, Mass., 1975).

Paper revolution in the Abbasid period:

J. Bloom, *From Paper to Print* (New Haven, 2001).

Print revolution in Muslim lands:

R. Bulliet, *The Case for Islamo-Christian Civilization* (New York, 2004), chapter 2.

Communications in Islamic history:

A. J. Silverstein, *Postal Systems in the Pre-Modern Islamic World* (Cambridge, 2007).

Chapter 2

Arabs:

R. Hoyland, *Arabia and the Arabs: From the Bronze Age to the Coming of Islam* (London, 2001).

Lewis, *Arabs in History* (as above).

Hourani, *Arab Peoples* (as above).

Persians:

R. N. Frye, *The Golden Age of Persia: The Arabs in the East* (London, 1993).

D. O. Morgan, *Medieval Persia: 1040–1797* (London, 1988).

R. G. Hovannisian and G. Sabbagh (eds.), *The Persian Presence in the Islamic World* (Cambridge, 1998).

Turks:

C. V. Findley, *The Turks in World History* (Oxford, 2004).

S. Soucek, *A History of Inner Asia* (Cambridge, 2000).

Chapter 3

Lord Clark on Greco-Roman architecture:

Lord Clark, *Civilisation: A Personal View* (BBC, 1969), episode 1: 'By the skin of their teeth'.

The mosque:

R. Hillenbrand, *Islamic Architecture: Form, Function, and Meaning* (Edinburgh, 2000).

M. Frishman and H.-U. Khan, *The Mosque: History, Architectural Development, and Regional Diversity* (London, 2002).

Jihad:

M. D. Bonner, *Jihad in Islamic History: Doctrines and Practice* (Oxford, 2006).

J. Kelsay, *Arguing the Just War in Islam* (Cambridge, Mass., 2007).

J. Esposito, *Unholy War: Terror in the Name of Islam* (Oxford, 2002).

The caliphate/imamate:

P. Crone, *Medieval Islamic Political Thought* (Edinburgh, 2004).

W. Madelung, *The Succession to Muhammad: A Study of the Early Caliphate* (Cambridge, 1997).

Chapter 4

Jean Chardin:

Jean Chardin, *A Journey to Persia: Jean Chardin's Portrait of a Seventeenth-Century Empire*, ed. and tr. R. W. Ferrier (London, 1996).

General:

R. S. Humphreys, *Islamic History: A Framework for Enquiry* (London, 1991).

C. F. Robinson, *Islamic Historiography* (Cambridge, 2003).

F. M. Donner, *Narratives of Islamic Origins: The Beginning of Islamic Historical Writing* (Princeton, 1998).

The Cairo Geniza:

S. D. Goitein, *A Mediterranean Society: The Jewish Communities of the Arab World as Portrayed in the Documents of the Cairo Geniza*; Vol. I, *Economic Foundations* (Berkeley, 1967).

A. Ghosh, *In an Antique Land* (New York, 1994).

Source-critical studies:

P. Crone and M. Cook, *Hagarism: The Making of the Islamic World* (Cambridge, 1977).

A. Noth and L. I. Conrad, *The Early Arabic Historical Tradition: A Source-Critical Study*, tr. M. D. Bonner (Princeton, 1994).

J. Wansborough, *The Sectarian Milieu: Content and Composition of Islamic Salvation History* (Oxford, 1978).

Idem, *Quranic Studies: Sources and Methods of Scriptural Interpretation* (Oxford, 1977).

Chapter 5

Sati' al-Husri quote:

A. G. Chejne, 'The use of history by modern Arab writers', *Middle East Journal*, 14 (1960).

Orientalism:

E. Said, *Orientalism* (London, 1978).

R. G. Irwin, *For Lust of Knowing: The Orientalists and their Enemies* (London, 1996).

Hodgson:

M. G. S. Hodgson, *The Venture of Islam* (as above).

M. G. S. Hodgson, *Rethinking World History: Essays on Europe, Islam, and World History*, ed. E. Burke III (Cambridge, 1993).

A. Hourani, *Islam in European Thought* (Cambridge, 1992), chapter 3.

Ibn Khaldun:

Ibn Khaldun, *The Muqaddimah: An Introduction to History*, tr. F. Rosenthal (Princeton, 1958).

Toynbee on Ibn Khaldun:

A. J. Toynbee, *A Study of History* (London, 1935), III: 322.

al-Tabari:

F. Rosenthal, *The History of al-Tabari: General Introduction and from the Creation to the Flood* (New York, 1989).

Chapter 6

Historical illiteracy amongst young Americans:

A. Ferguson, *Land of Lincoln: Advertures in Abe's America* (New York, 2007), Preface.

A traditional perspective on *Sunna* and the use of Islamic history by Salafis (both Islamists and Modernists):

A. Asfaruddin, *The First Muslims: History and Memory* (Oxford, 2007).

The Islam Channel:

www.islamchannel.tv

Wahhabism:

M. Al-Rasheed, *A History of Saudi Arabia* (Cambridge, 2002).

N. J. Delong-Bas, *Wahhabi Islam: From Revival and Reform to Global Jihad* (Oxford, 2004).

Religious development in Shiite Iran:

R. P. Mottahedeh, *The Mantle of the Prophet: Religion and Politics in Iran* (New York, 1986).

Khomeini on the rule of *mujtahid*-jurists:

H. Algar (ed./tr.), *Islam and Revolution: Writings and Declarations of Imam Khomeini* (Berkeley, 1981).

Martyrdom and Shiism:

D. Cook, *Martyrdom in Islam* (Cambridge, 2007).

Al-Qaradawi *Fatwa:*

www.islamonline.net (last accessed February 2009).

Chapter 7

Qays/Yaman:

J. Hathaway, *A Tale of Two Factions* (New York, 2003).

History and Arab nationalism:

A. G. Chejne, 'The use of history' (as above).

History and Turkish nationalism:

C. Hillenbrand, *Turkish Myth and Muslim Symbol: The Battle of Manzikert* (Edinburgh, 2007).

Kharijites in modern Egyptian political discourse:

J. T. Kenney, *Muslim Rebels: Kharijites and the Politics of Extremism in Egypt* (Oxford, 2006).

Islamic history in modern political language:

B. Lewis, *The Political Language of Islam* (Chicago, 1991).

The Golden Age of Spain:

M. Cohen, *Under Crescent and Cross: The Jews in the Middle Ages* (Princeton, 1994), chapter 1.

Conclusions

M. M. Khan, *The Muslim 100: The Lives, Thoughts, and Achievements of the Most Influential Muslims in History* (Leicester, 2008).

An alternative answer to this book's big question (widely criticized for its perceived anti-Muslim bias), is provided in: B. Lewis, *What Went Wrong: Western Impact and Middle Eastern Response* (Oxford, 2001).

Index

B

C

Index

R

THE KORAN
A Very Short Introduction
Michael Cook

The Koran has constituted a remarkably resilient core of identity and continuity for a religious tradition that is now in its fifteenth century. In this Very Short Introduction, Michael Cook provides a lucid and direct account of the significance of the Koran both in the modern world and in that of traditional Islam. He gives vivid accounts of its role in Muslim civilization, and compares it to other scriptures and classics of the historic cultures of Eurasia.

'Professor Cook's book is informative, witty, and rich with insight. The author firmly places the Koran within its broader context, lending his treatment depth and vigour.'
Mohamed Mahmoud, Tufts University

'This is a brilliant work of lucid scholarship and well-designed synthesis.'
Ian Netton, University of Leeds

www.oup.co.uk/vsi/koran